"It's my sincere belief that this book could not have come at a better time in the history of the church. In this hour, God is stressing that His heart for us is to understand our position as sons of the Kingdom so we can co-labor with Him to see a worldwide harvest. However, many of us need to reevaluate and understand how He has gifted us so we can come into the fullness of our position and learn how to move corporately as His redeemed Body. The Lord has anointed Ruthie Young to impart wisdom and passion to the Body of Christ to see the inheritance of our personal and corporate gifts unlocked, which is key to us receiving our full inheritance and walking in sonship! What is taught concerning Jesus encountering and overcoming every aspect of the stronghold set against each of these gifts is liberating and empowering. I am confident that God will use this work to release faith to you to arise and boldly lay claim to your birthright and to war to see it fully manifest for His glory!"

—**Charlotte Merschbrock**, Prayer Focus Ministries, LA Apostolic Prayer Network, Natchitoches, LA

"Ruthie Young's passion to see a believer's identity realized and destiny released for the glory of God is evident as she writes. There is such wonderful revelation and insight as she defines the spiritual DNA of the grace gifts, as well as issues that can hinder the gift in the believer. As you read, you are drawn into the heart of God and His manifold wisdom in creating and giving such extraordinary gifts to the Church."

—**Nancy Sleger**, Apostolic leader & Co-founder, Gulf Coast Community Church, Gulfport, MS

"Ruthie has accomplished a marvelous task. I was at the same meeting with her in San Antonio (even though we did not officially meet until a few years ago). For years I struggled with fully understanding the concept of redemptive gifts. She has made it clear, applicable and understanable. My heart swelled with joy as I read her words. I know

her well as a 'mercy gift' but she fulfilled the role of a ruler. I am a 'ruler gift' and her words sunk deep into my heart and confirmed once again my call: 'As world changers, Rulers, you finish what God has called you to do: build His Kingdom.' Ruthie did this through her work of love."

—**Dr. Thomas Schlueter,** Prince of Peace Church, Apostle and Pastor, Texas Apostolic Prayer Network, Coordinator

Your Destiny His Glory!

The How and Why of Your Design

Your Destiny His Glory!

The How and Why of Your Design

By

Ruthie Young

Copyright ©2014 Ruthie Young
Repairers of the Breach Ministries
P.O. Box 610
Corinth, MS 38835
All rights reserved
www.msrepairersofthebreach.com

All rights reserved. Any unauthorized reprint or use of this material is prohibited. No part of this book may be reproduced or transmitted in any form or by any means, electronic or mechanical, including photocopying, recording, or by any information storage and retrieval system without express written permission from the author/publisher.

ISBN-13: 978-1499647112
ISBN: 1499647115

The foundation of the information in this book comes from "The Redemptive Gifts of Individuals," Arthur Burk of Sapphire Leadership Group, www.theslg.com. SLG statement: "We have a passion to see our Great King establish His dominion over the whole earth. The various tools we offer all have that end result in mind."

Unless otherwise indicated all Scripture is quoted from the New King James Version®. Copyright © 1982 by Thomas Nelson, Inc. Used by permission. All rights reserved.

Other versions used where noted:
The Message Scripture taken from *The Message*. Copyright © 1993, 1994, 1995, 1996, 2000, 2001, 2002. Used by permission of NavPress Publishing Group.

ISV Scripture taken from the Holy Bible: International Standard Version®. Copyright © 1996-forever by The ISV Foundation. ALL RIGHTS RESERVED INTERNATIONALLY. Used by permission.

Cover Design by James Nesbit
www.jamesnart.net

Contents

Acknowledgements and Thanks	9
Dedication	11
Foreword by Sylvia Gunter	13
Foreword by Arthur Burk	15
Discovering My Identity	17
Your Destiny, His Glory!	23
The Gift of Prophet/Perceiver	35
The Gift of Servant	53
The Gift of Teacher	71
The Gift of Exhorter	95
The Gift of Giver	117
The Gift of Ruler	147
The Gift of Mercy	165
So What?	191
Lists of Sevens	197
List of Resources	199
Endnotes	201

Acknowledgements and Thanks

Very little in this book is original with me, but it is a compilation of thoughts, scriptures, and revelations from big-spirited pioneers filtered through my mercy spirit and put down on paper. So many teachers and leaders have done the "heavy lifting" on the study of the Romans 12 gifts. Others have added their perspective, all pouring into my life and experience to help shape who I am. To them I'd like to say 'Thank you!'

Arthur Burk, phenomenal mentor, teacher and friend. Our first meeting in San Antonio, Texas, literally shifted my life. Your understanding of the design of the mercy gift opened my spirit in a new way, launching me on a quest to discover, appreciate, and celebrate design— my design, the design of creation, the design of others— and to practice, ponder and savor the awe of our Creator.

Sylvia Gunter, you big-spirited, wonderful lady. You are a wordsmith of the highest quality. You have imparted wisdom and understanding of how to bless our spirits and given us beautiful, strategic words with which to do it. Your willingness to invest your time and input into this book has been "over the top!" Thank you!

Other teachers, Connie Fisher, Chuck Wale, and David Arnold, all brought a deeper dimension to my understanding of the Romans 12 or grace gifts.

Charlotte Merschbrock, my friend, my mercy counterpart, who kept saying, "You can do this." Thank you for your insight and willingness to read chapter by chapter.

Mildred Bean, always ready with the right scripture, you helped me see the great treasure in teacher gift.

Nancy Sleger, my spiritual midwife and "holy savage" prayer warrior, Thank you.

Erin and Phil Ulrich, publisher, friend, confidante. You planted the idea that a book was not an unreachable goal!

Deborah Brunt, my cheerleader and mentor in writing. You believed I could, and I did!

Mary Russell, my editor. You have shown me how to take an idea, put it into a complete sentence and communicate it in ways that actually make sense.

Marion Neil, your 'last minute' edit was of incalculable value to me.

James and Colleen Nesbit, for believing in me and for the cover art, thank you.

Rita and Mike Parks for freely opening your lake house to me for extended periods of time, and Mary and Shane for my time in your camper by the lake.

And a huge 'Thank you!' to all of my prayer warriors: My sisters Jimmie, Chalie, and Fran, Bunny Warlen, Delta Force, Betty, Sheila, and my CCF family, Lonnie and Annette, Katie and Danny. Danny, your blessings are over the top and my spirit soaks them up, thirsting for more.

And especially my children, Alyce and Chris, Mary and Shane, JoAnna and Rich, and Joseph. You have listened, been my Guinea pigs, prayed and encouraged me for years. Love you.

Dedication

To my soul mate, husband, and best friend, Billy Joe, ruler gift. I would have never had the confidence to begin this project, nor would I have had the push to "get 'er done!" without your support and encouragement. You have created a safe place for me, "had my back" and saw in me the potential for this book. I see in you the treasure of a true father in the faith, a mature ruler gift who understands how to nurture others as you build His Kingdom. I am eternally grateful to my Heavenly Father for bringing us together 43 years ago. It's been a fun ride!

Foreword
by Sylvia Gunter

Ruthie shines with a quintessential Mercy heart. Her Mercy heart for people feels deeply and longs for everybody to know their own God-given design and purpose and live the fullness of the abundant life that Jesus died to give them. She has lived the teaching on redemptive gifts over a decade of revealing its fruitfulness in her own life. She has been teaching the gifts for years with her own unique Mercy perspective. Now from the overflow of that rich experience she has written a book of deep rich treasure to be mined by all the body of Christ.

I think of Ruthie's passion for intercession. I first knew Ruthie and her husband Billy Joe as a formidable team of intercessors and passionate advocates for their beloved state of Mississippi. Few others have invested as much there. They are still intensely involved in seeing God fulfill all His design for the state, with all His plans and purposes coming to full fruitfulness. They are trusting Him for the harvest.

The word sterling comes to mind when I think of Ruthie. Great wisdom, maturity, and discernment are hallmarks of her life. She is genuine in every way and lives spiritual integrity of the highest order. Her personal life with God meets him where deep calls to deep. A relationship with Ruthie is always heart that meets heart and becomes iron that sharpens iron.

Ruthie is deeply committed to her family and stands in a line of generational faithfulness. Ninety nations have been impacted by four generations of her family … and counting.

Sylvia Gunter
Birmingham, AL
January 2014

Foreword
by Arthur Burk

Imagine two girls, each eight years old. One lives in a poor home in Minnesota. The other lives in a middle class home in Texas. Both receive a pair of ice skates for Christmas.

The difference in reaction will be immense. For the Texas girl, they are a novelty. She will need to go to the rink, learn how to skate and **decide** whether she likes ice skating well enough to fit it into her already happy, busy life. The skates might well be destined to be a marginalized toy, brought out once in a while on a whim.

Ah, but the little girl in Minnesota KNOWS what ice skates could do for her. She has watched the scarce money in the family go to buying skates for her brothers because they "need" them for hockey. She has ached for the skates and knows that now she can have fun, she can get out of the house, she can be with friends who skate, she can go like the wind and unleash the grace and intensity that is hidden within her.

She KNOWS what those skates mean for her whole childhood, and even though she will have a clumsy beginning, she is nothing daunted. She has been waiting and her passion overflows the banks, before she laces them up the first time. Now she CAN ...

This is a parable about Ruthie. Many people receive information about their identity and find it interesting on some level, like the girl in Texas.

But before she came across these tools, Ruthie knew in her spirit that there **was** a way for communities to be extraordinary, even though she had not seen it happen. When she found this teaching, her heart exploded with desire, knowing that people who walk in the dignity of design could produce the kind of community she always knew could and should be possible for Kingdom extravagance.

For the casual grazers, it is a book about technique.

For those with a heart to hear, it is a book about hope. It IS possible for community to do God-sized things. With these tools, the people of God CAN ...

Arthur Burk
Anaheim, CA
April 2014

My Journey
Discovering My Identity

Our great God is the ultimate gift giver. Throughout His word we discover He gives gifts. In the New Testament there are three specific lists of gifts, which we will look at more closely in the first chapter of this book.

I am a Mercy gift according to Romans 12. Knowing this, I have confidence in who I am, how I am designed, and why I see the world differently than others. I now understand my childhood, the desires of my heart, and my reactions and responses throughout life.

In addition, I perceive others in light of their own gifts. This perspective goes a long way in building unity in the Church. Before learning about the Romans 12 gifts, I assumed everyone saw the world around them as I did. Consequently, I was quite puzzled at their perceptions and reactions in different situations. Now, however, it is more clear to me that each person is designed by our Father to see the world through his or her own gift, viewing the same situation from one of seven different points of view.

Knowing and understanding my Romans 12 gift has shed light on circumstances from my childhood that were confusing to me. I'd like to share some of these with you.

I was told from a very early age that I was "slow." I did everything, whether eating, getting dressed, or reading, at a slower pace than the rest of my family. Not until I studied the gifts in Romans 12 did I realize that my being a Mercy means I am a watcher, an observer, a feeler. I enjoy savoring life and I transition slowly from one thing to the next.

Spiritual sensitivity is a strong trait of the Mercy, and he or she craves intimacy and spiritual fulfillment at a deep level. Growing up in the country, I walked a lot and was generally outside most of the time. Loving nature and talking to God came easily for me. As God and I had many specific conversations, my heart felt as if it would burst with love for Him. I always felt intensely connected to Him. However, when I tried to share this with others, I got strange looks. Therefore, I learned that this was a private place between the Lord and me, not something to be shared. In spite of this, every Sunday in Church, I continually yearned for something more, something deeper.

As a result, I tried a lot of "stuff" in high school, searching in many wrong places. Drawn to the occult, I found myself having séances "for fun." In my heart, I knew the supernatural dimension was real. In fact, when alone, I tried to "contact the other side," and, sure enough, I found I could do it quite easily. Did I worship Satan? No, I knew better than that, but I thought it was exciting to be on the edge of this vast spiritual realm.

I became a nurse and worked in Memphis, Tennessee, for three years, but I did not live a very godly lifestyle. The Mercy gift constantly seeks fulfillment in body and soul. Accordingly, one can turn to alcohol, competition, and sensual desires for this fulfillment. I was not immoral but skirted on the edge of all of these.

Then my soul mate, Billy Joe and I married after he returned from Vietnam. Following a tumultuous first year of marriage, we subsequently gave our lives to the Lord, received the baptism of the Holy Spirit, and entered the ministry.

Being able to play a guitar and sing, it seemed a natural fit for me to become a worship leader. Worship is the DNA of a Mercy gift. Through worship, I rediscovered the fulfillment I had experienced as a child. As I led groups into the Lord's presence, I was translated back to those times as a little girl when I had visions of heaven and of the

Lord, when I felt so close to Him, and when I was caught up into a glorious place of harmony and peace.

Billy Joe and I ministered in the Methodist Church for a few years before we joined a few others to plant Cornerstone Christian Fellowship, a Charismatic Church where I had the honor of being the worship leader. However, getting to Church on time with four young children, holding practice sessions with the worship team, teaching home school, and trying to help with pastoral duties became a little overwhelming, so I eventually left the team to focus on our life at home.

During this time at Cornerstone I heard about "motivational gifts" as taught by Bill Gothard. I learned that the Mercy gift is drawn to the brokenhearted as well as to worship. This was an "Aha!" moment for me. It explained why, all my life, there were wounded, precious people who sought me out in Church or at the grocery store or soccer matches. They would share their hearts and troubles with me; however, most of the time I could only respond with a hug because I had no answers.

Then approximately 12 years ago, through my husband's persistence, we drove 18 hours to hear Arthur Burk teach about "redemptive gifts," the study of gifts from Romans 12. Billy Joe had discovered this teaching and introduced me to Arthur's tapes. At this time, Billy Joe was traveling across Mississippi raising up prayer for revival in our state. Arthur's teaching about praying for land had piqued Billy Joe's interest, and the Lord had opened our eyes to His Kingdom coming in the earth. We were thirsty for more.

What we heard was amazing. About fifteen minutes into the first session, we looked at each other, totally overwhelmed. Have you ever tried to drink from a fire hose? We were both on overload and still had two days of teaching to go!

At the break, Arthur asked me how I was enjoying the session. I burst into tears, which was embarrassing, and said I was not coming back after lunch. There was just too much information. Arthur gently took my hands, looked into my eyes, and asked, "Are you a Mercy gift?" As I nodded yes, he made a statement that changed everything for me.

He explained that all other gifts process information with the mind. They categorize it, write it down, meditate on it, and internalize it before understanding it with the heart. But as a Mercy, I am different. I hear with my heart first, processing the information emotionally before filtering it to my mind. This session was too much information for my heart to absorb. Arthur's instructions were to put away the pen and paper and listen with my heart while asking the Father, "What is the one thing you want me to know?" It was simple, profound, and life-changing. For the first time, I felt validated in my unorthodox outlook.

Am I slow? No, I am a watcher. I observe, savor, and enjoy.

Am I weird? No, I was created not to "do" but to "be."

Are the brokenhearted drawn to me? Yes, I am like the mercy seat in the Tabernacle. The mercy seat is the place of healing.

Arthur's understanding of the seven gifts from Romans 12, which he calls redemptive gifts, has given me language to express what is inside my heart. It has helped me understand the lens through which I see the world and has opened up increased revelation for me in the Bible. I am comfortable in my own skin, and I have identity and legitimacy. I can now understand, love, and appreciate others because I understand me.

Thank you, Billy Joe, for seeing the value in this remarkable teaching. And thank you, Arthur, for exploring and developing it, for seeing the principles in the Word, and for going beyond the boundaries to discover deeper truths in the Lord. Thank you for building a platform for others like me to launch out from into new horizons.

Writing this book has been fun, exciting, hard work, and time consuming! I have loved it. I would like to make it clear that this is not a theological study even though I have strived to be scripturally correct. This volume is a personal attempt to connect the dots and principles from the Word of God to describe the seven personality types, or the gifts in Romans 12.

Understanding my design has given me confidence, insight, and a revelation of the Father's love for me. Therefore, it is my heart's desire to pass that understanding on to others, thus helping them in their quest to discover their identity, their value, and their unique design.

Chapter One
Your Destiny, His Glory!

You were Designed with Purpose and Destiny!

"So God created you in his own image.
Before He formed you in the womb He knew you.
His eyes saw your unformed body;
all the days ordained for you were written in His book
before one of them came to be.
How precious are His thoughts toward you.
How vast is the sum of them!
Praise Him, for you are fearfully and wonderfully made."
Paraphrased from Genesis 1:27, Jeremiah 1:5, Psalm 139:16-17, Psalm 139:14

There is no one else like you. No other person on earth has your specific genetic DNA code. You were created in God's image and formed by Him. As you were being shaped in your mother's womb, He placed His very own fingerprint into your DNA, a portion of His Spirit that no one else can replicate or copy. He wrote your destiny in His book before you came to be. Your design, His purpose. Your Destiny, His Glory!

In this book, we will look at, dissect, and discover on a deeper level the spiritual gifts listed in Romans 12. Earlier teachings taught that these seven grace gifts reflected our heart motivation, especially where ministry was concerned, and named them "motivational gifts." Arthur Burk renamed them "redemptive gifts" and expanded our understanding of this teaching. He explained how God uses this portion of His grace in our lives to bring us to maturity. Then we, in turn, can release His healing and redemption to the community around us.

There are three distinct lists of gifts found in the New Testament: Ephesians 4, 1 Corinthians 12, and Romans 12. The Ephesians 4 gifts are given by Jesus to the Church for the training and equipping of the saints in order to bring all Christians to maturity so we can fulfill the work of the ministry. The 1 Corinthians 12 gifts explain the manifestation of the Holy Spirit which is given for the benefit for everyone. The Romans 12 gifts are given by the Father on an individual basis, His fingerprint, His DNA, His grace in each of our lives. We will be examining and considering the Romans 12 list in this study.

Romans 12: 4-8 states: "For as we have many members in one body, but all the members do not have the same function, so we, being many, are one body in Christ, and individually members of one another. Having then gifts differing according to the grace that is given to us, let us use them: if prophecy, let us prophesy in proportion to our faith; or ministry, let us use it in our ministering; he who teaches, in teaching; [8]he who exhorts, in exhortation; he who gives, with liberality; he who leads, with diligence; he who shows mercy, with cheerfulness."

Throughout the rest of this book I will refer to the Romans 12 list as a grace gift, a Romans 12 gift or simply gift. This list includes Prophet, Servant, Teacher, Exhorter, Giver, Ruler and Mercy.

Gaining insight into your personal grace gift will lead you into new ways to interpret your response to the community in which you live. By community, I am referring to the people with whom you interact, family, friends, co-workers, and the people with whom you gather to worship, the Church. Fully embracing your gift will equip you to experience victory in some of the ongoing battles of your life where you have only seen temporary success. This insight can also help you accept and appreciate others as you see them function in their created purpose, thereby increasing unity in the Church. I pray this victory and discernment will become a reality for you.

The Manifestation of His Glory in the Church

When we are born again, totally forgiven, and cleansed by the blood of Jesus, we are changed. We have a brand new spirit and the perfect light of Jesus abides there. All things have become new.

Although Jesus lives fully in our spirit, the rest of our triune being—our soul (mind, will and emotions, our personality) and our body—must be renewed daily by the cleansing of His Word and revelation of His Spirit. In this portion of our three-part being our specific Romans 12 gift resides. Here our portion of His perfect light shines and reflects a specific color of His wisdom that we call our grace gift. And here we will focus this study.

Imagine a huge diamond, perfectly cut. Suddenly, a dazzling, pure, white light passes through this gem, and it comes alive with seven distinct colors. These rainbow colors are full of myriads of shades and blends, all dancing with light and brilliance. Jesus said, "I am the light of the world." As His light shines through us, we become alive with His light, reflecting one of those seven colors. That is His fingerprint in us, our one portion, our shade of His pure, white light which is our Romans 12 gift.

Through one of these colors we will view the world around us. For instance, if my gift is "red," then the entire world appears red to me. Conversely, if your gift is "blue," then you would see blue everywhere you looked. Prophet, Servant, Teacher, Exhorter, Giver, Ruler and Mercy. Seven gifts and seven colors of His light. Each one is distinct, but all together they make pure white light.

Let's look at Ephesians 3: 9-10 to get a glimpse of what this light might look like as the Church comes together to worship and seek His presence. The International Standard Version states: "He did this so that now, through the Church, the wisdom of God in all its variety (many colored, multi-faceted) might be made known to the rulers and authorities in the heavenly realm." In speaking of the Church here, it is referring to the gathering of Christians, followers of Christ. In this book when I use the word 'Church' I am referring to the Church worldwide, a small or large group gathered to worship the Lord, not a building made of brick and mortar.

As we manifest our own particular shade of His light, or our grace gift, we blend with others to show His wisdom in the earth as a new color of His luminescence. Rulers and authorities in the heavenly realm are watching. Gathering as the Church, we release this new combination of His supernatural wisdom or light. Heaven invades earth, principalities and powers are defeated, and the world sees our glorious, wise King.

Another analogy is found in John 17 as Jesus prayed for us to become one in unity with Him and with each other "that the world may know that You have sent Me." Discerning, embracing, and appreciating one another's grace gift helps eliminate competition and brings us into harmony with each other. This harmony produces a new blend of music the world is longing to hear: the sound of the Father's heart, the sound of the Church loving and working together in unity. The angels watch in amazement and the demons tremble with fear as Father releases His Kingdom to the earth in a new flavor, in a new blend of color and light, in a new key of music.

Understanding the Romans 12 gifts is only one of many tools our Father uses to bring about this symphony, but it is an excellent tool. It is the tool He placed in my hand, and I freely offer it to you in this book.

Benefits of Studying the Romans 12 Gifts

Arthur Burk asks two famous questions, "So what? What does it look like on Monday morning?" and he says, "God's secret weapon is love that works through community." [1]

Jesus told His disciples people would know us by our love for one another. As each of us come into the fullness of our created purpose, our destiny according to Jeremiah 29:11, we will be blessed, bless others, and the Kingdom of God will be evident in the world around us.

"That the world may know" should be the purpose of our lives. Understanding each other's grace gift gives us new building blocks to better understand those around us as we form community. We will have fresh perspective about how to live in partnership with others. This creates synergy, which in turn increases productivity in our relationships. But most importantly, we will reflect His grace, mercy, and love to a world in desperate need of His good news.

Your gift has equipped you to come into your destiny. When you were conceived, the Father gave you one lifelong "heart motivational" or grace gift. Satan has spent all of your life denying you the truth of this gift. Once you know and begin to move fully in your gift, you will basically discover who you are, who you were created to be, your place in the Church, and your portion that no one else can bring.

As we look deeper, we discover new treasures to be unlocked, new anointing of which we have been unaware. We gain new insight into our own strongest abilities and assets. This knowledge forges new weapons or tools to help us defeat our enemy who has come to steal, kill, and destroy us. As our discernment of his tactics increase, we begin to appropriate the blood of Jesus with new perspective, bringing an end to these tactics and increasing our authority in spiritual warfare. By knowing our portion and taking responsibility for that portion, our relationships in the Church, community, and work place should improve on all levels.

Life Experiences Which Affect Personalities

Many studies have been done and books written about personality traits and the way people respond or react to situations. Your grace gift is a huge part of your response. However, your response could also reflect other life experiences, such as wounding or abuse, immaturity, birth order, parenting, or genetic and hereditary factors. All of these circumstances come into play in forming your distinct personality, your uniqueness, and your response to your community. Therefore, your response in a given situation may be learned behavior, which does not reflect your gift.

For instance, a child raised in an emotionally abusive environment would certainly respond differently than a child raised in a stable home. This abused child might retreat into the background and be very obedient to authority, but move in a victim spirit. Similarly, the gift of Servant prefers the background and is fulfilled through serving others. The question is: "Does this behavior reflect the design of a loving Father bringing joy and fulfillment, or does it reflect fear of being noticed and drawing more abuse to themselves?" This is an example of learned behavior versus design.

In reading books about birth order, we learn that third children are usually gregarious, outgoing, and great fun to be around. They resemble the gift of Exhorter, who is usually an extrovert, too. Again, we need to discern learned behavior or design.

Another scenario that can mimic gift or design is parenting. If one parent is a Prophet/Perceiver gift, his drive for excellence can greatly impact his child, causing the child to become a high achiever. At the same time, however, the parent's influence may possibly instill the feeling that his child's effort is never good enough.

Some questions we might ask are: What is your heart motivation? What "lights your fire?" What is the area of your greatest fulfillment? These questions look beyond outward circumstances of birth order or environment and search deeper to identify design.

Excuse to Sin? Never!

As we continue searching into our design, can we ever use this gifting as an excuse to sin? Immaturity or carnality could cause us to exclaim, "I'm reacting out of my design, my Romans 12 gift. This is just the way I am." Does this justify disobedience to the Word of God? *Absolutely not!* We are called to imitate and become more like Jesus every day. He displayed to those around Him the image of His Father. He showed us how to live fully in our gift while never yielding to the temptation of sin. He gave us the blueprint to follow.

Although each gift comes with a negative side, Jesus always made a way of escape for us. There is power in His name to break every chain. As we reflect on these negative issues, we are always pointed back to the cross, the magnificent work of our Redeemer and the Creator who made us, loves us, designed us, then died for us. He made a way for us.

Discovering Your Grace Gift

Each gift has specific characteristics of behavior, which help us to easily spot and categorize them. However, we want to examine these grace gifts on a deeper level. We will look at the heart motivation, anointing, design, and the treasure hidden within each gift. We will also investigate unrighteous patterns and habits attached to each one and how our great advocate and champion, Jesus, made a way of escape for us from these chains of iniquity.

In each chapter we will consider some of the characteristics common to that grace gift and some of the Biblical characters who exhibited it. By analyzing their actions and responses from scripture, we can discern the design, motivation and even the battles common to that particular gift. Applying this discernment to our own lives, we hope to see our own gift more clearly and have some "Aha!" moments.

Jeremiah 29:11 says, "For I know the thoughts that I think toward you, says the Lord, thoughts of peace and not of evil, to give you a future and a hope." Our Creator has a distinct future, a destiny, and purpose for each of us. Although lived out in myriads of scenarios, there is a basic blueprint or foundational principle within each grace gift that reflects the potential destiny for individuals with that design. Salvation is a one-time, complete work of grace, but sanctification is a process. Our destiny, our birthright, is possessed in increments. Our birthright is our relationship with our Father as His son or daughter with all of the rights and privileges that comes with it. Our security is in who we are in Him. However, we must intentionally lay hold of the fullness of that and walk in responsibility to steward it. Embracing and maturing in our grace gift is one avenue the Father uses to help us possess our birthright in all of its fullness. His blood paid the price for our sin; His life showed us how we are to live after we accept that redemption. As we appropriate His victory over the stronghold blocking our own gift, little by little we will move forward to possess our birthright and destiny.

There are well over 100 "lists of sevens" found in the Bible. A partial inventory of these can be found at the back of this book in Appendix A. Our focus is the seven grace gifts found in Romans 12. However, when researching other "lists of sevens," our attention is drawn to the common characteristics and expanded understanding of corresponding numbers on each of these lists. The "lists of sevens" we will examine are: the seven days of Creation; the seven compound names of Jehovah; the seven pieces of furniture in the Tabernacle and the seven last words of Jesus on the cross, which will be discussed at the end of each chapter.

In Genesis one, each day of creation is filled with unique acts and attributes of the Father. As we study these, looking deeper for the principles found there, we begin to see how each day reflects a deeper revelation of the corresponding grace gift.

Our Great King cannot be limited by a name. He longs for us to know Him and have relationship with Him. Seven times in the Old Testament, He spoke His name prefaced by Jehovah. His name is so sacred the Israelites dare not even pronounce it. They called Him "Jah" or Jehovah, the sound of breath. It would be impossible to put into this space the full meaning of the name Jehovah. In fact, His name, His character can only be known in small increments because He is so wonderfully huge. He is incomprehensible and indescribable in the fullest sense of the words. A small definition of the name Jehovah is "the great supreme, sovereign Judge and God of the Universe, the Self-existent One, eternal, most vehemently holy Lord and Master."

As we study these seven compound names of Jehovah, God's heart is for us to discover more of His character. Serving Him is wonderful, but He longs for relationship. He created us to know Him, love Him, and trust Him as Father. Each of these names gives us a deeper, richer revelation of His loving nature. He is always good. As we look at each of these names in relationship to the Romans 12 gifts, we will see the correlation of His character as it meets a specific need in the corresponding grace gift.

When God met Moses on Mount Sinai, Jehovah gave him the blueprint for the Tabernacle, or large tent. Jehovah God would meet with His people in this Tabernacle, very intricate in its design. The pillar of cloud by day and fire by night hovered there as a sign to the Israelites that their God was living and was present. The word Tabernacle, a covenant word, means a permanent residence, dwelling place, or habitation. Each piece of furniture, the walls, the veil, and the coverings were elaborately designed and constructed with the finest materials, as we read in Exodus 25-27. Volumes have been written about the tabernacle with much deeper explanations than will be given here.

As a whole, the Tabernacle declared Jesus and His redemptive sacrifice. Every act of worship in this tent and each piece of furniture, from the Brazen Altar to the Mercy Seat, function to give us increased revelation of who Jesus is, what He came to do, and what He did for us on the cross. This book is not a study of the Tabernacle, but my hope is that something here might spark in you a desire to look deeper into this amazing picture of our Savior, Jesus Christ. In this study, we will look at each piece of furniture in the Tabernacle from the perspective of how it parallels a characteristic of one of the Romans 12 grace gifts.

- He is the sacrifice for our sin at the Brazen Altar.
- He is the Bronze Laver containing the living water that cleanses the priests and vessels and sets them apart for holy use.
- He is the Showbread, the Bread of His Face, the Bread of His Presence, and the High Priest who offers the blood sacrifice.
- He is the seven-fold Spirit of Light in the Menorah.
- He is our worship at the Altar of Incense.
- He is the Ark of the Covenant, which carried the jar of manna (provision), the Ten Commandments (the standard of holiness), and the Rod of Aaron (supernatural authority given by God).
- He is the Mercy Seat, the very presence of God.

Each gift carries natural instincts and abilities that come easily. However, there is one place, the deepest call and anointing for that gift, where we do not seem to be able to experience breakthrough. We call this the stronghold. There is a particular sin empowered by a root iniquity that creates this stronghold in a person's life. In looking at our specific gift, we will see that this one precise stronghold has haunted us all our life. We, in our own natural power, are completely powerless to break it. Only the blood of Jesus can reach deep enough to defeat this ploy of the enemy. Hidden deep within each stronghold is the glorious light of our destiny, our birthright and purpose of our grace gift, our design. Iniquitous patterns in our lives, like chains, keep us bound. Here the battle rages for our design to be released. There is power in the name and blood of Jesus to break every chain and set us free to run our race victoriously! Hallelujah!

We will see how Jesus identified each stronghold of the grace gifts on the cross and defeated it, thus breaking the iniquitous chains and unlocking our destiny. As we look to the cross for our individual battle, we will find our victory won and we are set free to live in the full capacity of our design. Is it a one-time battle? No. It is an ongoing war as we die to ourselves and are transformed into His image. This transformation process releases our unique color of His great wisdom in the earth, our design and destiny. That the world may know!

In considering the stronghold and root iniquity of each gift we must understand the difference between sin, rebellion, and iniquity. Sin is missing the mark. Rebellion is intentionally missing the mark. Iniquity is missing the mark so continuously until the sin and rebellion become a normal way of life.

Jesus manifested all seven of the personality or grace gifts to the maximum capacity. Analyzing incidents in His life which reflect each gift, we have a model of how it would look if we lived in the fullness of our own design, our grace gift.

His blood sacrifice was complete, paying the price for our sin 100%. His statement, "It is finished," reflects the completion of His redemption for the world. He had met the requirements as the perfect Passover Lamb, without spot or blemish.

Yet, before His death, as He walked through the agony of the cross, He was still completing His race in the earth as the perfect Lamb. Each of His statements reflects and conquers a precise stronghold found within each grace gift. In His most desperate last hours, He continued to show us the way to victory. In studying each of His last statements in depth, we recognize His obedience and His victory over our own specific stronghold as related to our grace gift. It is at this point we appropriate His grace. When we cannot live in victory at this point of our race, He did. He finished our race for us, and by embracing His grace we can more fully see how in our weakness He is strong.

Our Creator fashioned us with such care, exquisitely designing us with untold treasure. One tool He uses in our lives to deeply mine this treasure is our grace gift. By watching, discerning, and perceiving the best, the highest possible in a person, we can begin to see the treasure that God placed there. He calls us to search for it in ourselves and in others. As we discover this God-given treasure, we, too, will see the bigger picture, and learn to embrace His good and perfect design in ourselves and others.

In the portion designated 'the treasure' I have tried to paint a picture of what we might look like if we walked in our design according to our grace gift. This is a goal to be desired. Some say, "If we aim for the stars, we might hit the moon." But I say, "If we aim for the stars, with the supernatural power of our Great God, we might just hit the stars!"

Selah!

In the Book of Psalms we find the word "Selah!" which means to stop, pause, and reflect. As I wrote this book, many times meditating on the goodness of our awesome God, I would literally stop for a few moments to worship, weep, laugh, and even shout. One day as I wrote about the expanse of stars and lights in the sky, I was in such awe of His hugeness and brilliance that I began to laugh. As I read what I had written, I was amazed that my hands continued to type as my heart and mouth praised Him. Somehow, I wanted to convey this emotion, so I left the words I had written but prefaced them with Selah! I had paused, reflected, and worshiped the Lord because of the fresh revelation of His Glorious Majesty. I hope you experience a few "Selah's!" throughout this book. And may your life be blessed with many Selah! moments.

Chapter Two
The Gift of Prophet/Perceiver

"It's black or white, right or wrong! End of discussion."

Have you ever held a conversation with someone who has made these statements? If so, you were probably talking to a person with the Prophet/Perceiver gift.

As we discuss this grace gift, remember we will not be talking about the verb "to prophesy" as 1 Corinthians 12 nor the five-fold ministry gift of prophet from Ephesians 4. Here we are examining the Romans 12 gift of Prophet/Perceiver.

The Greek word prophet (prophētēs) means one who predicts, foretells, or makes known. Perceiver means one who discerns, recognizes, distinguishs, grasps, comprehends, judges, or adjudicates. Understanding and implementing the black and white principles of truth enable the Prophet/Perceiver to extend the truth into the future. He can predict the outcome, not by supernatural means, but from simple deduction. If it worked here, it will work there. By understanding principles from the Word of God, the Prophet/Perceiver can know in advance what will happen. In most of our discussion of this grace gift, we will shorten Prophet/Perceiver to Prophet.

Prophet/Perceiver Characteristics

- The Prophet holds a simple worldview. To him, it is either right or wrong, in or out, black or white.

- The Prophet can take something apart, put it back together, and many times it will work better because he sees the design and understands the principles involved in the process.
- A natural leader, he is very bold, not easily intimidated, usually the first to jump out in front with solutions to problems, and knows no fear.
- Verbally expressive, he is a great communicator with prolific speech. Recognizing the truth and processing the facts immediately, he sees the long-range plan and declares it. Believing he is always right, most of the time he is.
- The Prophet rapidly assesses situations, is quick to war and fast to take initiative. He may shift gears without warning. We call this 'changing lanes without giving a signal.'
- Fiercely competitive and carrying a passion for excellence, he is never satisfied with a job less than well done.
- To the Prophet, "Truth is truth!" Honesty and a high level of integrity are extremely important for him. He is hasty to judge people, sin, or situations if he perceives any breach of integrity. He will readily break relationship if complete disclosure is not offered. The standard is the same, whether a casual friend or a person with whom he has a deeply committed relationship, he requires total, complete honesty. Maturity comes as he studies the principles of relationship and chooses to listen rather than judge, build bridges rather than walls.
- Although his tendency is to judge quickly without all the facts, he is just as quick to forgive and restore when full disclosure is offered.
- This visionary is always looking ahead and must feel he is going somewhere either around the bend or the next great adventure.

- Everything must make sense to the Prophet. He wants to know the 'why' of all situations. Learning to say, "I don't understand, but let God be God" is another sign of maturity.

- Having the widest range of emotions, he can rapidly sink into dark depression but just as quickly experience great joy or deep compassion. The Prophet is usually transparent about his own faults, passes the harshest judgment on himself, and is quite willing to suffer for truth.

- His deep desire for justice and his inability to tolerate bondage in himself or others drives the mature Prophet to see others set free from the slavery of sin. This is paramount to his character.

- Unable to "turn off" his tendency to judge or improve matters, he goes through life thinking, "This would be better here, that would work better if they did this…"

- He likes to fix things, frame them, and move on to something new. Terrible at maintaining the status quo, he will enlarge it, change it, or quit it.

Prophet/Perceiver Characteristics as Seen in Bible Personalities

Peter, John the Baptist, Naomi, Ezekiel, and Caleb all exhibited characteristics of Prophet. Let's take a deeper look at two Biblical characters in particular, Peter and Caleb.

Peter

Peter's compulsiveness as well as his quickness to take initiative and recognize truth led him into some extreme situations. He jumped out of the boat and walked on the water. It was he who shouted, "Let's just build a tabernacle!" and declared, "I'll go to the death for You, Jesus."

Coming on the heels of his brave declaration of loyalty to Jesus, Peter's denial caused him deep despair. After his repentance, he was still left with great guilt. These examples from Peter's life reveal his wide range of emotions and his impulsiveness.

Jesus certainly understood Peter's desperate need for forgiveness and relief from the guilt he carried. After the resurrection, Jesus specifically said, "And tell Peter ..."

When Peter preached the first evangelistic sermon on the day of Pentecost, he nailed it. This Prophet could see clearly the design of salvation. He was the first to declare the finished work of Jesus in the earth, setting the precedent for evangelistic outreach. He had neither the "Roman Road to Salvation" scriptures nor the gospels as a guide. He had Torah, the books of the Prophets, the teachings of Jesus, and the Holy Spirit. As a follower of the Jewish law, he had celebrated Passover every year and had seen the principles laid out in Torah and the Passover celebration. Pulling these principles together with his long-range vision, he clearly saw the design of salvation and redemption. He preached these truths on the day of Pentecost. Peter's Pentecost message is a first-class example of the high calling of the grace gift of Prophet. The Prophet is gifted to see the principles in the Word of God, understand in advance what they should look like, and then declare them to the world.

Once again, true to the design of Prophet, Peter chose the most difficult kind of death for himself, embracing pain for the sake of the Kingdom as he was crucified upside down.

Caleb

Another grace gift Prophet, Caleb, mighty warrior, saw the potential of the children of Israel moving into the Promised Land by God's power and authority. He understood the principles of truth. If God said it and did it in Egypt, then God will do it for us in Jericho. Boldly standing alone in the face of a whole nation of unbelievers, Caleb had the faith to believe and declare it. Because of Israel's unbelief, Caleb had to embrace the pain of waiting for the next generation to bring the nation of Israel into the Promised Land. After forty more years in the wilderness, still standing firmly in faith and true to his Prophet gift, this mighty warrior asked for the most difficult land, Mt. Hebron, the mountain of the Lord. His cry was, "Give me the land of the Giants!"

Prophet/Perceiver's Foundational Principle: Design

Understanding how the principles of God and nature work every time, then using this information to solve problems brings joy and fulfillment to the Prophet. He discovers new ways of doing things and finds innovative approaches to difficult situations. His call is to see long and deep into the Word of God, identify the principles, then make application of those principles to bring solutions and answers for the Church.

Knowing that something works is not enough for the Prophet; he must know why it works. Seeing design gives him confidence to know and replicate it in other settings. Because he saw the design of God's relationship with men throughout the ages, Peter could easily understand and embrace how the Church would function in the present day. With his profound ability to communicate it to the people on the day of Pentecost, he brought the old principles forth to conceive this new thing: the Church. He understood the principle of forgiveness Jesus modeled on the cross and applied it to bring freedom, first to himself, and then to the new believers.

Prophet/Perceiver's Birthright: Faith to Move from Bondage to Freedom

Faith comes easily for the Prophet because he sees and understands principles, and he knows they will work every time when applied. For instance, the principles of natural law such as the law of gravity, the law of aerodynamics, and the laws of thermodynamics never change. Neither do the principles of truth, salvation, and redemption. The redeemed Prophet sees God's principles in His Word, and in full faith understands that God's laws will work every time. Thus, because of his boldness and lack of fear, he is willing to step out to declare the end results of these principles.

Freedom and justice are core values of the Prophet. Knowing the principle of freedom through the blood of Jesus never fails, the Prophet can see what the finished product will look like. Through his amazing ability to convey his message, he casts this vision for others to see. By applying this principle to his own life, he is willing and even eager to embrace the pain in order to taste this wonderful liberty and deliverance.

Helping the Church understand God's design of salvation and redemption, the Prophet can inspire others to push through their pain to obtain their own freedom. His deep desire for justice and his inability to tolerate bondage drive him to become life-giving and to bring others into restoration. Painting a picture of how full restoration might appear, he gives hope to the hopeless and becomes a rebuilder of the broken.

Lists of Sevens

We will explore four of the "lists of sevens" found in scripture. For more information and a partial inventory of these lists, please see Appendix A. The Prophet/Perceiver is the first on the list of gifts found in Romans 12. Accordingly, we will examine each correlating "first" on the other "lists of sevens" to discover information and insight pertaining to the Prophet/Perceiver gift.

First Day of Creation

Genesis 1:1-5. "In the beginning God created the heavens and the earth. ²The earth was without form, and void; and darkness was on the face of the deep. And the Spirit of God was hovering over the face of the waters. ³Then God said, 'Let there be light'; and there was light. ⁴And God saw the light that it was good; and God divided the light from the darkness. ⁵God called the light Day, and the darkness He called Night. So the evening and the morning were the first day."

On the first day of creation there was no structure, only abstract darkness and void. There are three different words used for darkness in the Bible. The darkness of Genesis 1 is defined as misery, destruction, death, ignorance, sorrow, wickedness and chaos. This darkness covered the face of the waters. This darkness also covered Egypt with a plague. And, finally, this darkness appeared at the cross the day Jesus died. Natural sunlight, a candle, a floodlight, or the light of our own lives cannot penetrate this darkness.

What was in God's mind as He hovered and brooded over this darkness? What was it He saw as He looked from the end to the beginning? Did He see your face? Was His heart excited or broken as He saw creation unfolding? Did He feel joy or sorrow? I believe our Great Creator God felt both joy and sorrow as He longed to love and be loved by a people created in His very own image. The joy the Creator felt was the same intense joy that parents feel when they peer deeply into the eyes of their firstborn child.

Yet, deep sorrow also came as God looked ahead to see the plan of His enemy who would come to kill, steal, and destroy His beloved children. Did He see the agony of the cross as the price required for His children to live in freedom as sons and daughters? Did He see the anguish and suffering of His only Son, the Son of His heart, the Son who **was** His heart? He had a decision to make as He brooded. Gazing intently toward His Son and then toward His children, God made His choice, "just as He chose us in Him before the foundation of the world…" (Ephesians 1:4). He made the choice of a broken heart, a choice only a loving Father would make. For God so loved the world that He gave. He chose us.

He spoke and light came into the world.

Selah! I must stop and declare what an awesome, magnificent God of love, compassion, and power we serve! He loved us so much He gave His heart, His life, His son.

The books of Hebrews and 1 Peter both tell us that Jesus Christ was slain from the foundation of the world. Was it at that moment the light of creation was released? When God spoke, "Light," was His only Son sacrificed at that moment? Was it then the true Light of the World pierced this deep spiritual darkness? Was His Son the only Light that could penetrate such evil, chaotic blackness? I am not a theologian, nor do I propose to have the answers to these questions, but I do wonder. Our noble King knew the price to redeem creation before He created it, and He still chose to say "Yes." Yes to the price. Yes to the pain because He loved us already and deemed us worthy of the supreme sacrifice, the life of His only begotten Son, Jesus.

Our God saw the complete design of creation before it ever came to be. He saw it all from end to the beginning. He embraced the pain. Light shattered darkness, and Creation was born. And God saw that it was good.

As the first in the list, the Prophet is the one who sees design. If you, reader, are a Prophet gift, then you share with the Creator Himself this portion of His image. All are made in His image, but you carry this portion of His unique light, the ability to see design end from beginning, and declare the new thing into the earth. You see outside the box. Your portion is to conceive new things and grasp spiritual truths on a deeper level. When your spirit is alive with His spirit, you will have more creative ideas than you will know what to do with. Therefore, it is essential you spend time getting to know our Father, our Creator, and what He has called you to do. Then you will know which of those creative ideas are to be brought into fullness and which ones you are not called to do.

After He finished His creation, God stepped back and said, "Now THIS is good!" And in this too, Prophet, you can identify with Him. Because of the high standard of excellence you carry, you will hear His words echo in your spirit, "Job well done!"

First Fruits Offering

First fruits offering is an important concept for everyone, but especially for the Prophet gift, because he is the first fruit of the list from Romans 12.

Here are some scriptures about first fruits offerings:

"When you come into the land which I give to you, and reap its harvest, then you shall bring a sheaf of the first fruits of your harvest to the priest." Leviticus 23:10

"All the best of the oil, all the best of the new wine and the grain, their first fruits which they offer to the Lord....Everything that first opens the womb of all flesh, which they bring to the Lord, whether man or beast." Numbers 18:12,15

"Christ the first fruits." 1 Corinthians 15:23

First fruits offerings were commanded in the law of Moses. This offering was not for sin. The nation of Israel was commanded to give the first of their crops, flock, time, and resources. Even the firstborn son was set apart as holy and required an offering to "buy him back." Although we have much teaching in our churches about the tithe, the first 10% of our money, I believe that there is much more to be discovered about first fruits.

Time was created on the first day. What you celebrate first is your priority. So, Prophet, why not extend this first fruits principle to all areas of your life? Celebrate time. Celebrate the first fruit of the New Year, the first day of the month, the first hour of your time in the morning. Celebrate the first fruit of your joy, sorrow, good news, and pain. When any wonderful, exciting thing happens to you, don't call your best friend to tell him. Celebrate the first fruit of joy with your Father. Shout, dance, and laugh with Him, then call your friends. Do the same with sorrow. Don't call the prayer chain first. Turn your heart immediately to the Lord and worship Him simply because He is worthy to be praised and worshiped, even in the midst of deep despair.

I've witnessed in my daughter's life the advantage and spiritual authority that comes for the Prophet who sanctifies the first fruit of time and even the first fruit of frustration. Interestingly, as I was writing this portion about the Prophet, she called to tell me about her day of great frustration. Events of the day had compounded, and I was amazed that all of this could happen in only one day. During our conversation, we chose to become grateful for the good things in her life and to offer first fruits of frustration. Her circumstance did not change, but she did. The desired peace and assurance came, assurance that our Father is still in control. Because she loves Him and is called according to His purposes, she knows that He will work all things for her good.

Jehovah-Jireh

Genesis 22:8, 14. "And Abraham said, "My son, God will provide for Himself the lamb for a burnt offering… And Abraham called the name of the place, The-Lord-Will-Provide; as it is said to this day, 'In the Mount of the Lord it shall be provided.'"

"God will provide Himself, the lamb." Many times when we invoke the name of Jehovah-Jireh, we are focused on His provision for our material possessions. As we look more closely, Jehovah Raah or Rohe, our Shepherd, is the one who supplies our physical needs. Jehovah-Jireh is directly related to the sacrifice of the lamb, the precious Lamb of God who takes away the sin of the world.

We discussed how our Father chose to sacrifice His only Son. Here Abraham was asked to do the same. This is a life or death situation and such a beautiful picture of our redemption, the complete work of the blood of Jesus.

For the Prophet gift, this is a black or white issue. Forgiveness versus unforgiveness. Freedom versus bondage. All or nothing. Pure grace. No one can earn it, buy it, nor embrace enough pain to attain it. As the Prophet learns to receive this grace, he sees the principle of freedom exhibited. Isaac was totally set free by the blood of the ram in the bush, and we are totally set free by the blood of the Lamb of God. As the Prophet embraces the freedom of forgiven sin, his astounding ability to communicate this principle brings restoration and life to others. He sees clearly the principle of freedom by the blood of Jesus, and he is quick to declare this truth to all who will listen.

The Brazen Altar

The Brazen Altar is the Place of Sacrifice. Entering the outer court of the Tabernacle, the Prophet is immediately halted by the brazen altar. He can go no further. At this altar sin is confessed and the penalty for sin, death, is paid. Full repentance is required, followed by the death of the sacrifice, and then by full forgiveness. As the daily sacrifices at the Brazen Altar were being made, the aroma of burning flesh and fat smelled like forgiveness to the children of Israel. It was not a pleasant smell, and it was a very costly one. To the Prophet, this smell is the fragrance of freedom.

At this altar, the Prophet is designed to react more strongly than others. He sees the need for genuine repentance with full disclosure of sin before forgiveness comes. A free gift of forgiveness may be difficult for him to accept. Because of sin in his own life and his drive for excellence, God's way seems too easy. He may be demanding of others, but he is so much more demanding of himself.

The Priests had to offer sacrifices to cleanse the altar and cleanse themselves first. Only after this process could they stand before the Lord to offer sacrifices for the people. The Prophet must live in that standard of holiness first, receiving full forgiveness for his own sin before he can demand it for others. This requirement of full disclosure of sin before forgiveness applies to all.

Because he sees long, God has given the Prophet the vision to see beyond the Brazen Altar all the way to the Mercy Seat. He sees the sin altar and the death required. Yet looking past this altar he is able to see the full design of the tabernacle, complete restoration of the sinner. He sees the laver for cleansing, the showbread for intimacy, the menorah for light, and the incense for worship. Beyond the veil with the flaming swords embroidered on it, he sees the Ark of the Covenant, which is the Father Heart of God and the Mercy Seat for intimacy in His presence.

Those flaming swords are a reminder of what was lost in the garden, as the Lord stationed cherubim with flaming swords to close the way back. The Prophet recognizes that beyond the veil, the Mercy Seat is where full restoration of relationship with our Father/Creator takes place, the relationship that goes all the way back to the garden.

But there is more. The Brazen Altar was not just for the sin offering. At this altar the guilt offering, thank offering, and praise offering were presented.

Our Father knew that the Prophet gift would understand the principle of the sin offering. Perceiving the Prophet's desire for justice and excellence, God also knew the Prophet would leave the sin altar feeling he had personally failed to meet the standard. He would leave carrying guilt, the kind of guilt that kills. In His compassion, the Father required a second offering called the guilt offering, the place of closure. At this same altar the Prophet must make a second sacrifice and leave his guilt at this altar too. Through this second offering, he would learn the difference between conviction and condemnation. "There is therefore now no condemnation to those who are in Christ Jesus." Romans 8:1. There is full forgiveness and full restoration. No guilt. No condemnation for failing to meet the standard. When the Prophet could not meet the standard, Jesus did.

Our loving Father didn't stop there. He loves to celebrate. With this new freedom comes celebration. At this altar the Prophet presents a thank offering and a praise offering too. It is difficult to continue to rehash sin and condemnation with an attitude of gratefulness and praise. As his eyes focus on the goodness, love, and kindness of the Father, the Prophet's heart leaps for joy, and he comes into a deeper intimacy with Him as he experiences this freedom.

One more thing: the first fruits offering is given here too.

Selah! So, whoop it up, prophet! This is what you were created to do. Where others sniff burning flesh, you smell freedom. You smell restoration. You smell holiness, thanksgiving, and high praise. Celebrate it! Show us what first fruits of all of these sacrifices look like. We need to see His glory in a new shade of light and hear His heart in a new key of music: freedom!

Prophet/Perceiver Stronghold and Root Iniquity: Fractured Relationships and Not Respecting the Rights of Others

Do you want to identify an unredeemed Prophet gift? Check out his track record. There will be relationship after relationship after relationship, all broken. Check out his usual thought process, "This was not my fault. If he would admit he's wrong, explaining what he did wrong, I would certainly continue to have relationship with him."

At the Brazen Altar, full disclosure of sin is required, and the carnal Prophet requires no less than full disclosure of any wrong that may have been committed against him. He is quick to forgive, but only if the offending party makes a complete confession of his wrong and asks for forgiveness. Sometimes even that is not enough to satisfy the unredeemed Prophet. And one more chain gets wrapped around the treasure chest carrying his destiny, and the lock gets stronger. That, my friend, is a stronghold—the stronghold of fractured relationships.

The root iniquity that keeps this stronghold locked down tight is not respecting the rights of others, even their right to make mistakes. How well the prophet embraces relationships will be a major factor in the basis of his fulfillment in life. Only at this place can he discover his purpose—freedom and restoration for himself and for others caught in bondage.

Talking more than he listens, the carnal Prophet lacks tactfulness in rebuke, exposes without restoring, and tends to cut off people who fail. Feeling that his standard is the one to meet, he can hold unforgiveness, carry bitterness, and dwell on the negative. Constantly looking for the "new," he tends to move from relationship to relationship without full reconciliation. Holding more tightly to principles than to relationships, he has great difficulty with intimacy, both on the spiritual level with God and on the emotional level with men or women. To the Prophet, this feels normal, and the iniquitous pattern is well established. Remember, sin is missing the mark; rebellion is intentionally missing the mark; but iniquity is missing the mark to the extent that it feels normal. Believe me, this Prophet is not a warm fuzzy!

Time with Father

Breakthrough comes only by time spent with our Father. Allowing God to work in his weakness builds a platform for the Prophet's strength. He must earn the right to speak by listening, to God first, then to others in his family and community. Understanding principles is his strong suit. Therefore, it is imperative that he begins to study the principles of relationship and learn to build bridges rather than to cut ties. Intimacy comes hard for the Prophet, but it is not impossible. As the Prophet develops his relationship with God, allowing Him to soften his heart, the Prophet can allow himself to be vulnerable and open his heart to the people around him.

Offering first fruits of time to Him is an excellent way to pursue intimacy with the Father. Embracing rather than just teaching the principles of covenant is crucial. And the Prophet must never embrace bitterness.

All of this sounds great, but for the Prophet it is impossible to attain. Releasing forgiveness without full disclosure? Refusing to embrace bitterness when you have been wronged or wounded?

What happens when you, Prophet, cannot forgive, when you cannot mend broken relationships because you have been so deeply wounded by those who will not hear what you have to say? What happens when you cannot break the chains of iniquity because of the bitterness you harbor in your heart?

Jesus, our Champion, made a way for you. He conquered and opened the way for you to welcome and accept the fullness of your destiny. He broke the chains of fractured relationships, broken covenants, and bitterness. He came to set you free.

Jesus as Prophet/Perceiver

Identifying with the Prophet gift when He was on earth, Jesus understood the design of creation, fallen man, and redemption. He willingly embraced the pain of the cross to bring full restoration to creation. By expelling the moneychangers in the temple, He held to a righteous standard. He did everything with the spirit of excellence and extravagance. When He turned the water to wine, it was the finest wine, more superb than the father of the bride could afford. His drive for justice and intolerance of bondage caused Him to release many who were enslaved by demonic spirits. He saw the end from beginning and brought full restoration to Zacchaeus and to the woman caught in adultery. He knew Judas was stealing, but He forgave without confession to keep His relationship open. Yes, He understood you, Prophet. He walked in your shoes.

The Last Words of Jesus on the Cross: "Father, forgive them."

The Prophet's passion for holiness drives him to require justice. The soldiers, not realizing their prisoner was the perfect Son of God, treated Him cruelly and unjustly. At his most vulnerable time Jesus received no justice.

Prophets are verbal and quick to speak. Our Champion spoke "not a word."

Prophets require full disclosure, confession, and repentance before forgiveness is released. This never came for our Savior.

Jesus saw the bigger picture, that this was God's plan. The offense came by the Father's hand, as does any offense against us. Prophets become offended at God and are prone to bitterness toward Him. But Jesus held no bitterness. He refused to break relationship, even without full disclosure of the offense.

Jesus saw the design and cost of freedom. He understood the principle of death on the Brazen Altar, the death of the ram in the bush, and the death at the foundation of the world. He was willing to embrace the pain of the cross to pay the highest price, the price His Father required—a cruel and unjust death.

Seeing the end from the beginning, Jesus looked down through eternity and saw you, strong Prophet. He saw that you could not release the forgiveness, embrace injustice, refuse the offense, or push the bitterness aside. He saw you trapped in a stronghold of broken relationships. He says to you, "You could not, but I did!"

"Father, forgive them, they don't know what they are doing"

These words echoed throughout eternity. Jesus gave full forgiveness without full disclosure.

He gave full restoration for all sinners, even if they never embrace it.

Mercy? Extended.

Grace? Offered freely.

He forgave the Roman soldiers for the injustice.

He forgave the Jewish high priest, Peter, and even Judas for their betrayal.

He forgave His Father for the offense that came. This covenant relationship held firm.

My! What a Savior!

Selah! Oh Magnificent Savior! In our weakness, you make us strong, you complete what we cannot! You do the impossible so that we can move in the supernatural! Forgiveness extended!

So I say to you, Prophet, embrace the work of the cross for you. By His blood, you are forgiven and set free. By His words, you appropriate that freedom.

The Treasure of the Prophet/Perceiver

As you are functioning through the Spirit of Jesus living in you, you smell like freedom and justice. You are a defender of spiritual freedom, and you see the full design of salvation from Brazen Altar to Mercy Seat. You are known as a restorer of the broken, a spiritual father or mother, and a man or woman of faith who carries others from brokenness to freedom.

Your ability to see outside the box, discern principles, and deduce outcomes enables others to comprehend and embrace their highest call. You speak it, and we see it. Casting the vision of restoration, you lead us toward it, bringing hope to the hopeless. Your high standard of excellence encourages others to look further and aim higher.

Always running ahead, you open paths for others to follow. Arriving first, you call back and encourage us, showing us that we, too, can make it. With your warfare anointing and drive for integrity, you have the capacity to shift political systems, bring justice to the outcast, repair the breaches, and mend the broken.

Prophet, we need your portion of light and your key of music. We embrace the treasure the Father has revealed in you.

Chapter Three
The Gift of Servant

The delightful lady at Church who comes in early to make the coffee, brings the flowers, and takes care of the nursery when others do not show—what is her name? The older gentleman who seems to know where everything is, and if you need a picture hung or the grass cut, he's your man. But what is his name? These Servant gifts have a name, but most people do not remember it. Taken for granted, these wonderful, essential people are always there to help everyone else do their job. They are unappreciated, and the rest of us have missed the rich treasure hidden inside them. The Servant is truly a "gift" to the Church.

Servant Characteristics

- Loyal, tenacious, and life-giving are a few words to describe the person with the gift of Servant.

- Without asking questions, the Servant is quick to obey, quick to see, and quick to meet practical needs, such as comfort or food. In general, he enjoys serving. With his life-giving words and perseverance, sinners feel loved by the Servant, and leadership is blessed by his attentiveness to detail.

- The persistent Servant finds it almost impossible to give up on needy people. He will go the limit, even using his own resources to continue to draw the 'hard cases' into the Shepherd's fold.

- He enjoys being a team player and thrives on specific assignments, which allows him to empower others.
- Uncomfortable with attention, he is usually in the background and prefers to stay that way. His acts of service are his voice. This attribute carries much weight in the spiritual realm, and he can calm a storm and shift the atmosphere simply by stepping into a room.
- Never yielding to a slave or victim mentality, a redeemed Servant extends the physical ministry of Jesus in the earth with great intention for eternal purposes.
- Because he finds it difficult to set parental boundaries, the Servant can enable his children to become prodigal. Feeling he is their last hope, he will continue to say "yes," giving and giving until he has depleted his own resources in trying to help, usually to no avail.
- Although passive when offended himself, the Servant becomes a tiger when the one he loves is offended. Nevertheless, his own passivity toward offense can produce bitterness in his heart.
- The Lord can trust the Servant with great spiritual authority, especially in life or death situations, because the Servant is not an empire builder and is without guile.
- The Servant makes an excellent armor bearer for leadership. His desire to make others comfortable and his willingness to go the extra mile by screening phone calls, intercepting noncritical issues, and taking care of appointments gives the leader freedom in his schedule to devote time to other priorities. However, this is only the tip of the iceberg for the armor bearer Servant. His impact in the spirit to stand in the gap for leadership is unprecedented. When the redeemed servant understands his authority and prays for leadership, the results are historic. Please note the story of Daniel Nash later in this chapter.

- Others may take advantage of the Servant because he is willing to serve so unselfishly. Without affirmation from those he serves, a slavery or victim mindset may develop, causing him to embrace verbal abuse and even use self-deprecating language. The fact that others do not remember his name only serves to validate this mindset.

- As an intercessor many times he has a passion for praying over land and is often associated with cleansing, water or agriculture issues. He exhibits high spiritual authority when praying over land and the atmosphere.

- Collecting, saving, and holding on to possessions, the Servant may have difficulty throwing objects away for fear he might need them some day. Having these possessions seems to help him feel safe and he can see their usefulness and possibilities when others might deem them worthless.

- Servants seem to step up when needed and then disappear into the background after the job is done.

Oh, how we need the gift of Servant!

Servant Characteristics as Seen in Bible Personalities

Jonathan's armor bearer, no name given, Ananias who prayed for Saul, Jesus' earthly father Joseph and Esther (her Hebrew name was Hadassah), all displayed this gift. We will study Joseph and Esther more closely. Although not a Biblical character, Daniel Nash is a picture of how a servant intercessor can shift a city.

Joseph, earthly father of Jesus

When we hear the name "Joseph," we automatically think of Jacob's son Joseph, who became the assistant to Pharaoh. Overlooked most of the time, Joseph of Nazareth, the carpenter, was a Servant who was very quick to obey, loyal, and extremely life-giving. He was handpicked by God and entrusted with the life of God's own son. What an honor. What a responsibility. This Joseph stepped up when his name was called and stood between life and death for Mary and Jesus.

God said, "Joseph, Mary is pregnant, marry her." And he did.

God said, "Joseph, although she is nine months pregnant, take Mary to Bethlehem." And he did.

God said, "Joseph, the king is attempting to kill the baby. Get up quickly and go to Egypt." And he did.

Demonstrating his authority over life and death, Joseph saved Mary from being stoned and shielded Jesus from King Herod. Through his loyalty to Mary, he created a safe atmosphere for the Son of God to be brought into the earth. We will really never know what happened to him, because after his time of serving, Joseph the carpenter, this quintessential Servant, disappeared from sight.

What a splendid picture of the Servant gift.

Queen Esther

Queen Esther moved in great authority over life and death also. Orphaned at a young age, Hadassah lived with her cousin Mordecai. He must have done an amazing job because she never seemed to live in an orphan spirit. When conscripted by the king's authority as a candidate for queen, Esther trusted and obeyed Mordecai explicitly and kept her Jewish heritage a secret. Without guile, she won the favor of the eunuch who had charge over her and, eventually, the favor of this pagan king.

Esther was quite attentive to the King's likes and dislikes. I'll bet she knew how he liked his coffee, his favorite dessert, and his preferred perfume. Her loyalty to him and her desire for his comfort gained her great honor and approval. She became the apple of his eye.

She may have been orphaned as a child, but this dedicated Servant knew her destiny and understood her authority. She was a queen. Risking death, she courageously entered uninvited into the king's chambers. Capturing his heart by her extraordinary gift of hospitality, she set the atmosphere for life and saved a nation in a day.

But there is more. Looking ahead to Nehemiah, her influence can still be seen. As Nehemiah approached King Artaxerxes about returning to Jerusalem, the king quickly gave permission and also authorized the supplies needed to rebuild the wall around the city. Could the king's willingness to offer help to the Jewish nation have been the influence of his step-grandmother Queen Esther? I believe it did. God trusted her with great authority and her influence could still be seen affecting the next generation.

Daniel Nash

Almost everyone knows the name Charles Finney, the marvelous revivalist, evangelist, and man of God. But hardly anyone has ever heard the name Daniel Nash. As I was just beginning to understand intercession for whole cities, the Lord put a small pamphlet into my hands about this little-known man. I was quite intrigued as I read his story. This quiet, unassuming man with a Servant gift was a good friend and personal intercessor for Charles Finney, Exhorter gift. We have heard the stories of Mr. Finney as he entered a city to hold evangelistic meetings. People on the sidewalk fell in repentance, and transformation came to the entire area. His mass meetings were historical, as this fiery man of God preached salvation. Factories would shut down when he entered, because a strong conviction of sin would be released onto the workers. But no one mentions Daniel Nash.

Working as partners, Mr. Nash and Mr. Finney prayed together to hear the word of the Lord as to which city would be next. Mr. Nash would then enter this city weeks before the scheduled meetings. Taking a room in a boarding house, he would spend days weeping, fasting, and praying in order to set the atmosphere for spiritual life to be released. The Irish call it a "thin place" where heaven comes down so close to the earth that breakthrough for healing and salvation happens easily. Daniel Nash prayed until the "thin place" was evident.

He paid a price for this kind of intercession. A boarding house owner called Mr. Finney one day to report she suspected his friend, Mr. Nash, was quite ill. She mentioned he hardly came down for meals, his light was on most of the night, and she heard strange groans and moans coming from under the door. Mr. Finney assured her that Mr. Nash would be all right as this was his usual custom. At some point, Mr. Nash would send a note to Mr. Finney declaring, "The city is prepared and ready."

As Mr. Finney entered the city, miracles happened, revival broke out, and the Kingdom of God was mightily advanced in what we now call the Great Awakening. And where was Mr. Nash by this time? He had moved on to the next city, already preparing the way, breaking the ground, and setting the atmosphere for the King of kings Himself to enter the city. As a result of such prevailing prayer, heaven invaded earth through the words of Mr. Charles Finney.

This is a stunning example of Servant gift, a man with no fame but who embodied great authority, set the atmosphere for life to spring forth throughout an entire region.

Within a few months of Mr. Nash's death, Charles Finney left the evangelistic ministry and took a position as pastor of a church. The Servant intercessor was gone and the partnership was over. Now we know the rest of the story.

Servant's Foundational Principle: Legitimacy and Authority

"Knowing who you are because of who your Father is" is the call for the Servant gift.

The understanding of the Servant's position in Christ is foundational to his ability to embrace and live in the authority the Lord has given him concerning life and death. The Servant must know two facts. First, he must know his Father is the Great King of the Universe. Second, he must know he is the son of this Great King.

From this position of sonship, he lives in great authority in his Father's Kingdom. Because of his identity as a child of the King, he is called to live with secure borders, protecting and releasing life through words and actions. This life of authority and identity creates a safe atmosphere for healing and cleansing to take place.

The Servant is called to live in such legitimacy that he will step up when his gift is needed but his name is not called. Hadassah, better known as Queen Esther, stepped up in full authority to release an atmosphere of life to save her people, even when her name was not called.

Servant's Birthright: Favor with Secure Borders

Coming alongside leaders, stepping into the gap of life for restoration of families, and cleansing of defiled land are some of the realms of authority for the Servant. But the Servant must hear from his Father the one thing he is called to do. Living with secure boundaries, having the confidence to say "no," and choosing the important rather than the urgent are marks of a redeemed Servant who lives in his design and purpose.

Second Day of Creation

Genesis 1:6-8. "Then God said, 'Let there be a firmament in the midst of the waters, and let it divide the waters from the waters.' Thus God made the firmament, and divided the waters which were under the firmament from the waters which were above the firmament; and it was so. And God called the firmament heaven. So the evening and the morning were the second day."

On the second day, God created the atmosphere. The assignment of the atmosphere is the task of maintaining life. On this day, boundaries were established and life-sustaining, cleansing cycles were set into place.

Invisible, yet beautifully calibrated to sustain life, the atmosphere is essential and complex. Constantly in motion, the clouds move vast amounts of water, protect from the sun, cleanse from pollution, and continuously release life. Lightning strikes keep the earth from losing its electromagnetic charge and release 10 million tons of nitrogen into the soil per year, thereby fertilizing our plants. One small shift in the oxygen/carbon dioxide ratio, and life would cease to exist. The daily amount of sunlight dictates the capacity of plant growth and even impacts our emotions. Yet, it all goes unnoticed, **taken for granted**, unless there is a tornado, flood, or hurricane.

Such invisibility certainly reflects the Servant gift. Mirroring the unseen yet essential effects of the life-giving qualities of the atmosphere, the Servant carries an immense authority to cleanse and bless the land, to cleanse and bless leaders, to live in authority over the death spirit, and to release a safe place for the wounded to receive healing and life. As a cloudy or sunny day impacts our emotional state, the Servant, who is the most stable emotionally, affects the spiritual climate for the rest of the gifts, especially as we gather to worship as the Church.

God celebrates and identifies with the Servant gift. He is usually taken for granted, too, and is not appreciated for the magnificence of His gifts and life-sustaining presence. Others may take the Servant for granted, but He does not. He notices. Father celebrates and honors the Servant.

Selah! I am humbled and grateful to such a superb, loving God! And I take notice of the behind-the-scenes, constant, amazing, life-giving atmosphere! And for the wonderful, life-giving, self-sacrificing

Servants I have been privileged to know and love. My grandmother, Mama Grace, was one of these. She prayed for me.

Jehovah-Rapha

The compound name of Jehovah-Rapha was given at the cleansing waters of Marah in Exodus 22. As soon as the children of Israel grew tired and thirsty in their journey, they began to complain to Moses. Consequently, the Lord led them to bitter water. Directing Moses to a specific branch, God instructed His leader to throw it into the water. When Moses obeyed, the water became sweet.

Historically, the water at Marah was white rather than muddy or clear. It contained the minerals, magnesium and calcium. Here God told the Israelites that none of the diseases of Egypt would follow them. He revealed His name as Jehovah-Rapha, the Lord your healer or the Lord your health-keeping God.

In Egypt, both the Israelites and their animals drank water from the Nile River. They washed their clothes in it, took their baths in it, and probably still carried parasites from it. Facing the ominous task of crossing a desert, which would be a long, hot trek across scorching sand, God brought them to the bitter waters of Marah. Dry and thirsty, they all drank some of this water, even though it was very bitter.

Are you familiar with the effects of magnesium on our digestive system? It will cleanse your system. And so it did to the Israelites. Just a small amount of this mineral water sent them running to the latrine, wherever that was in the wilderness. Not pleasant, but quite effective to rid the body of parasites.

Drinking this water would also have put large amounts of magnesium and calcium, better known to athletes as dolomite, into their bodies. Long distance runners use this supplement to keep their muscles from cramping as they sweat, especially for long treks crossing hot deserts with scorching sand.

Get the picture? God was using the bitter water to cleanse their bodies and prepare them for a desert crossing. Preparing them for a new diet, a new way of life, He would give to them living water rather than the parasite-infested, slow-moving Nile River. He would give them new ways to stay healthy and prepare them for what was ahead. He was their health-keeping God. He promised "If you will... Then none of these diseases will come upon you."

If you will obey Me, if you will follow My laws, if you will keep My covenant, then I will keep you healthy, whole, and prepared for any difficulty that lies ahead.

The unseen Servant helps keep the Church healthy by taking care of small details. Embracing bitterness, doing dirty jobs, loving the hard to love, and seeing and meeting needs, the Servant performs all these tasks behind the scenes. He is unnoticed, taken for granted, and yet so essential to keep the Church ready, moving and prepared for what is ahead.

At one time or another, we all come to bitter waters. By creating a safe atmosphere of hospitality, releasing living water through his words and actions, the Servant can prepare a place for others to find healing and comfort in the middle of difficult circumstances.

The Bronze Laver

The Bronze Laver, probably the largest but the most overlooked furniture in the Tabernacle, stood at the door of the Holy Place for the cleansing of the sacrifice and the priests. It consisted of a large bowl or fountain, which held fresh water and stood in a base to catch the wastewater, much like a huge cup and saucer.

Some of the holy furniture could become defiled if someone or something unholy touched it. Not so with the Laver. Any article or person touching it was re-cleansed and made holy again.

The dirty, messy business of animal sacrifice was not a pleasant sight, nor did it smell very good. But it was necessary. Here at the

The Gift of Servant

Laver the sacrifices were washed and prepared for the Brazen Altar. Following this duty, the priest had the honor and privilege of going into the Holy Place into the presence of the Lord. The Bronze Laver made possible the transition from sacrifice to a place of sweet-smelling fragrance and beauty.

An armor bearer for ministry leaders is a reflection of this picture, and none do it better than a Servant gift. He instinctively seems to help make this transition possible. His cleansing quality can determine how deep the leader may go into the presence of God. When men came back from war, they were commanded to go to the priest to be cleansed physically, emotionally, and spiritually before going home to their families. Sometimes ministry feels like war. The Servant has the highest anointing to cleanse leaders from the cares, wounds, and emotional exhaustion of ministry by taking care of the essential but oftentimes consuming details.

Just as water purifies, dilutes, cleanses, and refreshes, the Servant can create a holy atmosphere for the leader by preparing the place, by fielding phone calls, by clearing his schedule, and by praying for him. This allows the leader to come into the presence of the Lord for longer, more frequent periods of time. All of the body benefits from the excellent cleansing of the Servant. Taken for granted? Probably. Essential for spiritual life? Absolutely!

Servant Stronghold and Root Iniquity: Victim Spirit and Peace at Any Cost

Failure to embrace the truth that God is my Father and He supplies all my needs creates in the Servant the strongholds of a victim spirit and hopelessness. It is easier for the Servant to believe Satan's lie that he is a worthless nobody who deserves all the ridicule and abuse that come to him. Believing this lie leads to an incapacity to trust God to take care of his provision and needs, especially in his family.

Many times the Servant believes he is the only one who can or will take care of the needs he sees around him. Saying "Yes" to everything and being unable to set solid boundaries, he will strive to keep the peace, regardless of the cost to him mentally, emotionally, spiritually, and even financially. In other words, he becomes an enabler. Many children of Servants become prodigal because, just as he is unable to set his own boundaries, the Servant is also unwilling to set boundaries for his children.

Let me say here, Servant, your name is not Jesus! Only He can fulfill His promises to take care of everyone's need according to His riches in glory.

The servant's inability to set boundaries for his time, resources, and even personal space attracts a predator spirit which comes to steal, kill, and destroy the Servant's self worth and any other portion of his life that is available.

When offended, his passivity can lead to bitterness, anger, and self-loathing. Believing he doesn't really count, the Servant waits for someone else to validate him before he will assume his place in the Church. He is bound by this illegitimate victim spirit, which affects the rest of the Church. By refusing to embrace the authority given to him by the Lord, he fails to shift the atmosphere from death to life.

Time with Father

There is only one way to break the chains that keep the precious treasure locked inside the Servant. Time spent with his Father. Spending time with Him is the only avenue to fully know Him, His face, and His voice. Trusting God's character of loving-kindness and tender mercy, the Servant can depend on his Father to meet his needs and the needs of those around him and also to set secure boundaries for him.

As the servant begins to believe that he is truly God's child, the lie of illegitimacy fades. He can begin to rise up and accept the authority given to him, because his Father has validated him. No longer plagued by an illegitimate spirit, the Servant can begin to live in his true identity as a legitimate son. True legitimacy is knowing who your Father is and knowing who you are because of who your Father is. From this position he can empower others, know when to say "yes," and know when to set the boundary around himself with a well-placed "no."

But, Servant, what happens when situations demand your gift, but you feel so illegitimate, worthless, and insignificant you cannot step up? What happens when you have been so victimized and wounded that you choose to shrink back into the shadows, believing you deserve all you get? How do you break out of the chains of bondage that have cost you everything? You are spent, bruised, and beaten. And there is no one around to lift you up.

Jesus, our Advocate, made a way for you. He came to bind up the brokenhearted and set the captives free. A bruised reed He will not break. He sees the treasure inside of you, and only He has the key to unlock your prison and set you free.

Jesus as Servant

Jesus changed the atmosphere of the whole world in a day.

Constantly challenged by those in authority, Jesus lived in authority in every situation, refusing to embrace what others said about Him. He was possibly told He was illegitimate when He was a child. After all, the neighbors knew that Mary was pregnant when she married Joseph. Without honor in His hometown, He heard the taunts of people when they said, "Can anything good come out of Nazareth?" Yet He knew He had the authority to forgive sin.

He knew who He was, He knew where He came from, and He knew where He was going, so He could take a towel and wash His disciples' dirty feet. John 14:3-5.

He controlled the atmosphere and spoke to the waves. Life-giving in all He said and did, He raised the dead, healed the sick, and released deliverance to the captives.

Above all, He knew the one thing He had come to do. Jesus saw needs around Him constantly. He could have spent years and years healing the sick and raising the dead. He could have spent days feeding the hungry by multiplying food. And He really could preach good sermons! Thousands would come to hear Him. But this was not what He came to do. Jesus said "No" to all that could have distracted Him and set His face like flint toward the Cross. He chose to do only what He saw the Father doing and speak only what He heard the Father say.

The Last Words of Jesus on the Cross: "Today you shall be with Me in Paradise."

At nine o'clock in the morning, just as the Passover lamb was placed on display by the high priest for all of Israel to see, Jesus trudged through the street naked for all of eternity to see. He was exhausted, beaten, and bloodied beyond human limits. Spit dripped down His face, skin was torn from His back, and the crown of thorns was pressed into His temples. He was the Son of God, yet the world saw a common criminal being punished.

"If You are God, save yourself."

"How can You save the world, if You can't save yourself?"

Did He hear someone from Nazareth say, "He's just the illegitimate son of Mary!" Or someone from Capernaum sneer, "He's no good, only a worthless, itinerant preacher."

His friends? Nowhere to be found.

Only the jeers of the religious leaders and taunts and accusations from the demons in hell reached His ears.

When the whole world was against Jesus, what did the thief on the cross see or hear that gave Him the courage to ask for mercy from this dying man? Did he hear Jesus ask His Father to forgive those who were crucifying Him? Did that statement spark hope in this condemned criminal that he, too, could possibly obtain mercy? What did he see in Jesus at that moment that caused him to request such a thing? Luke records that this thief shouted to the other thief, "Can't you see He is innocent!" Then turning to Jesus, he asked, "Lord, remember me when You come into Your kingdom."

Did his request ignite something deep inside Jesus? I believe it did. I believe He looked down through eternity and He saw you, Servant. He understood as never before what illegitimacy felt like, smelled like, and tasted like. He had nothing to validate who He was or what He came to do. No friends, no money, no clothes, nothing. When all the world said He was nothing, a nobody, He refused to believe this lie from the pit of hell. He remembered who He was—the Son of the Living God, Creator of the Universe. He remembered where He came from—heaven's glorious throne. And He knew where He was going—back to His Father's embrace. He recognized the extraordinary authority the Father had given Him, authority over life and death.

At that moment, He knew this day He had authority over life, death, and hell. And this day He chose life. Turning to the thief, He released that life by saying, "Today you will be with me in Paradise!"

Jesus knew who He was when the entire world said He was nothing.

He knew what He needed to do, and he stepped up to do it when no one called His name.

He was suspended in the atmosphere, to shift the atmosphere, excellently calibrating it for life.

He created a safe environment for the presence of His Father to come and be present. That was hospitality at its finest.

He embraced the bitterness and defilement of the whole world and cleansed it according to John 3:16.

He knew the one thing He was called to do. He did it, and He did it well.

At the place where you, Servant, cannot embrace your legitimacy, He did it for you. When you are desperate for validation, He validates you as only He can. As you bow your knee at this place of the cross, appropriating His blood and embracing His legitimacy for you, your chains are broken. This key unlocks your prison of victimization. You are set free with secure boundaries to do the one thing you have been called to do— partner with Him to set the atmosphere for life to be released.

Selah! Marvelous, glorious Savior!

The Treasure of the Servant

God chooses men and women to release His character, His miracles, and His life into the earth. Servants, no one does it better or stronger than you. As you walk in favor, allowing the Father to set your boundaries, you possess authority for cleansing the land, the atmosphere, and leadership. Healing of the family unit, ecological restoration, and high authority over the death spirit are your playing fields.

Your tenacity in modeling the gospel is unparalleled, and your incredible anointing for hospitality and cleansing prepares the way for leaders to move into their own destiny.

Getting to know the Father intimately, what He likes, what draws His presence, and being so connected to both the earth and heaven realm, you, Servant, can open a portal for a "thin place." "Thus says the LORD, 'Heaven is My throne, and earth is My footstool: where is the house that you will build me? And where is the place of My rest?'" Isaiah 66:1.

With your supernatural gift of hospitality, you, Servant, can set the atmosphere for His presence to rest. Rise up into your destiny to create a resting place for the King Himself. The world needs to see and experience the fragrance of His beauty and holiness, to be drawn into intimacy with Him. No one creates this holy atmosphere as well as you. You have the anointing, creativity, and understanding of the atmosphere of holy hospitality just like Esther.

So, come out of the kitchen, in from cutting the grass, and take your honored seat at the table of the Lord. We, as the Church, need you, honor you, and celebrate you.

Chapter Four
The Gift of Teacher

The truth, the whole truth, and nothing but the truth! Truth is the call and the playing field of the gift of Teacher. The Teacher's firm grip on the plumb line of truth helps us as Christians to remain doctrinally sound. Feeling he must validate it, validate it, and validate once more to make sure this is truth, the Teacher is like the proverbial snapping turtle if others oppose what he is convinced is truth. He won't turn loose until it thunders. Please understand, the Teacher gift does not mean he must teach. This is the way he views the world, not an activity in which he participates.

Teacher Characteristics

- The Teacher will not quickly embrace or reject a new idea or proposal but will ponder it, analyze and authenticate it before he makes a decision to accept or reject it.

- Because of his need to verify and consider all sides of an issue before speaking, the Teacher may appear passive. In a meeting he will quietly listen to all sides of an issue, contemplating it before bringing words of wisdom to the discussion usually at the end of the meeting.

- To some the Teacher appears passive, but more than likely he is pondering, validating, and analyzing the issue. He must then make a choice. Sometimes the Lord calls him to confront the issue and make a stand. If the Teacher chooses not to take the action required after this deep inner deliberation, he can move into a spirit of passivity, which negates his effectiveness. However, when the redeemed Teacher rises to confront, the results can be spectacular. Note Daniel's confrontation later in this chapter.

- Slow to make decisions or judgments, he is a safe person for emotionally hurting people. Because he is comfortable around brokenness, his gift can be confused with the Mercy gift. He can also be mistaken for a Prophet because of his strong-willed, inflexible stand for truth.

- The Teacher is great fun to be around, has deep family loyalty, and usually has a good sense of humor. Slow to move, he partners easily with others and balances the impulsiveness of the Prophet and the Exhorter gifts.

- If he becomes puffed up over his knowledge, he will at times argue over minor points and will only accept teaching from those who have credentials he respects.

- The Teacher relies strongly on factual evidence, so he is uncomfortable with any issue until it is proven. He finds it hard to accept by faith new moves of God or new teachings. He finds safety in documenting and validating. When God moves in new, unprecedented ways, the Teacher will usually wait, watching to see if it can be historically documented or found in the Word.

- The Teacher finds great pleasure in revealing the truth, line upon line, precept upon precept, especially to those he loves. One of his greatest joys is to plant this truth in good soil and then watch with delight as it grows and bears fruit.

- Since he is non-confrontational and prone to yield to a spirit of passivity, the Teacher has difficulty imposing responsibility on others. He will make numerous excuses and see many reasons why it is not a good idea to ask a particular person to take responsibility in any area, especially if that person is already busy. A pastor with this grace gift might see a sin such as adultery in his congregation, yet he will refuse to confront it. Preferring to teach a series about the destructiveness of adultery, he will not confront the adulterer or ask him to assume responsibility for his sin.

- He likes connecting the old ways to the new and seems to enjoy historical facts and old things. If it's tried and true, he appreciates it.

- How do you walk on water? You must know where the stepping stones are placed. When the Prophet/Perceiver walks on water, he skips two or three stones and gets to the other side quickly, usually alone. The Exhorter may jump to the first, second, and fourth stones, then dive in and swim to the other side with a gang of merry followers. But the Teacher will deliberately step on each stone, slowly and methodically. His concern is for others who are following, to make sure they have a solid stone on which to step. Why is this important? As God moves in the earth in new ways, the Prophets/Perceivers are usually the first to embrace or reject it. Exhorters will run with it, bringing many others along. The Teacher watches, moves slowly and documents each step in order to give others a firm foundational authority on which to step. This helps to keep the Church historically and doctrinally sound. As God moves in new ways, the synergy of these three gifts is very important.

Teacher Characteristics as Seen in Bible Personalities

Ezra wrote 1 and 2 Chronicles; Mary pondered things in her heart; Samuel was loyal to house of Saul; Luke validated specific times of

Jesus life. Others with the Teacher gift were Levi and the Levitical priesthood as a whole, Isaiah, and Daniel wise advisor to pagan kings. We will contemplate Luke and Daniel.

Luke

Thank you, Dr. Luke. Truth and validation are central to the DNA of the Teacher gift and Luke validated. Because he accurately recorded the circumstances surrounding the birth of Jesus, we can pinpoint the time of this historical event. Luke makes clear "the when, where, and how" of the birth and early childhood of Jesus. This information probably came from Mary the mother of Jesus, another Teacher who pondered and kept all of the circumstances hidden in her heart. Here are some of the specifics from the Gospel of Luke:

- While Zachariah, a priest of the division of Abijah, was serving in the temple, he received the message that he and Elizabeth would have John the Baptist. Carefully kept Levitical records can document this date.
- Herod was King, a historical record easily traced.
- The World Tax was required. The government kept accurate tax records.
- Caesar Augustus was ruler.
- Quirinius was governing Syria.

Luke wanted everyone to know Jesus' birthplace and His lineage.

- Bethlehem
- Joseph was of the House of David
- Joseph was of the Tribe of Judah

Did it really matter? Was this important? Yes, it was. Remember, Jesus said not one jot or tittle would be missed. Luke's information documents several prophecies from the Old Testament, including the one from Micah that Jesus would be born in Bethlehem. The tax records would show that Joseph would have had to go there to pay his tax, because he was of the tribe of Judah and was a direct descendant of David.

Luke documented the burial place of Jesus as the tomb of Joseph of Arimathea.

Although we in the Christian faith accept the Old and New Testaments as the Word of God, this historical documentation proves to be important to people outside our faith. Luke gives us concrete proof that Jesus lived, died, and rose from the dead. Luke documented it in his gospel and validated it by historical and governmental records.

Daniel

Daniel knew God through the study of the Jewish Law as a child. Taken captive to Babylon at a young age and recognized for his education and wisdom, he was chosen to be a part of an elite group of young men educated in Babylonian culture. When asked to break the Jewish dietary laws and eat from the king's table, Daniel listened for the purpose of this command. Realizing the issue was the health of this chosen group and not the food itself, his appeal to authority based on wisdom rather than direct confrontation achieved great results. The Lord honored this young man by allowing him to keep the Law and still remain in favor within the Babylonian governmental system.

Daniel influenced ungodly governments through his reputation for wisdom and dream interpretation. Continuing to increase in wisdom and favor, he gained the trust of the pagan rulers Nebuchadnezzar, Belshazzar, and Darius.

Daniel understood how to legislate government from the heavenly realm rather than by navigating the political system of Babylon and Persia. As we observe his prayer life, we see he discerned the will of God by fasting and prayer. Through his God-given wisdom, he was able to legislate the Kingdom government into earthly government.

For instance, he learned from scripture the captivity of the Israelites was to last 70 years. It was now time for the exiles to go home. He went into his prayer chamber, fasted, prayed, and declared it until a message from heaven was sent to him that his prayer had been heard and answered. He had brought the decree from heaven's throne room into the earthy realm. Shortly thereafter, the government gave permission for the Jewish people to return to Jerusalem.

To Daniel, it was quite simple: God was the sovereign King, and Daniel was His ambassador on the earth. The Babylonian and Persian kings were merely players in the hand of his King. God revealed to Daniel His will for the Jewish people on the earth. Daniel's position was to fill the intercession gap between heaven and earth until he saw the evidence manifest in the earth realm. His prayer was the same as Jesus taught us to pray: "Thy kingdom come, Thy will be done, on earth as it is in heaven." The governmental anointing of the Teacher allowed him to move in wisdom, to understand how Kingdom government works, and to partner with the King to see His rule come in the earth as it is in heaven.

However, in the life of the Teacher, there comes a time when he must push past his desire to remain passive and actively confront issues to release the will of God into the earth. Daniel recognized when active confrontation became necessary. Not being swayed by the gifts offered to him and realizing that this king could take his life with a nod of the head, Daniel confronted Belshazzar. Instead of passively reading the handwriting on the wall, Daniel stood up to this young king face to face. Explaining how God had blessed his father Nebuchadnezzar, Daniel declared that he, Belshazzar, had offended the God of heaven and defiled the holy vessels of the temple through idol worship. The outcome was spectacular! Rulers died and nations shifted. Belshazzar was killed that very night, and a new Persian king took over. Daniel was awarded the gifts promised from the Babylonian king, and he was elevated to a new level of governmental authority in the kingdom of the Medes and Persians.

Teacher's Double Portion

Throughout the study of the Teacher, we discover a double portion, a twofold application that resides in all areas, from the foundational principle to birthright, from the third day of creation to the words on the cross, and all the way to the root iniquity. This double portion is unique to the Teacher gift.

Teacher's Foundational Principle: Responsibility to God and Man

The foundational principle for Teacher gift is responsibility. It plays out in two applications and reflects the two greatest commandments given by Jesus: to love God and to love others.

First: to love God with all of your heart, soul, mind, and strength.
1. To intimately know the God of Truth, not just the Truth, worshiping Him in spirit and in truth.
2. To understand His Kingship and declare His government in the earth.

Second: to love your brother as yourself.
3. To understand the need for social justice, becoming proactive in the affairs of men.
4. To require others to step into responsibility.

This is depicted beautifully in the priestly garments. These garments were blue cloth woven with gold thread. Depending on how the light fell on the cloth, the skirt first looked blue, representing man, and then appeared gold, representing God. Having a twofold purpose, the priest stood before God on behalf of the people as they worshiped Him. Then, turning to the people, the priest stood in front of them on behalf of God to release judgments, forgive sin, and pronounce Aaron's blessing, thus illustrating the Teacher's responsibility toward God and man.

Teacher's Birthright:
To Understand the Deep Truths of God and Declare His Kingship in the Earth

The birthright of Teacher gift is twofold. First, he must know, teach, and demonstrate the deep truths of God. These truths reveal God's manifest presence to the world. The revelation of His presence requires intimacy with God. Since the Teacher cannot release to the others what he does not own, he must first know the God of Truth, face to face, at a deep-rooted, genuine level.

Daniel, who knew God on an intimate level, demonstrated the second portion of the Teacher's birthright. He moved in wisdom to reveal God's Kingship and facilitate His government in the earth. Daniel functioned well in the Babylonian and Persian cultures because he knew that his King ruled over them all.

Third Day of Creation

Genesis 1:9-13. "Then God said, 'Let the waters under the heavens be gathered together into one place, and let the dry land appear'; and it was so. And God called the dry land Earth, and the gathering together of the waters He called Seas. And God saw that it was good. Then God said, 'Let the earth bring forth grass, the herb that yields seed, and the fruit tree that yields fruit according to its kind, whose seed is in itself, on the earth'; and it was so. And the earth brought forth grass, the herb that yields seed according to its kind, and the tree that yields fruit, whose seed is in itself according to its kind. And God saw that it was good. So the evening and the morning were the third day."

On the third day, God was busy. Land appeared, the seas were gathered together, and trees and plants sprung to life.

Flowers popped up everywhere—vibrant purple iris and orchids, white magnolias, pink roses, fields and fields of bluebonnets and yellow daffodils. Lush vegetation of every type covered the earth, including gloriously green trees and vines hanging with fruit of every kind, reflecting the splendor of the imaginative, artistic King we serve.

How does this parallel the Teacher gift? We have two events taking place. Dry land appeared, and then came the vegetation, flowers, trees, and herbs. The best part was He pronounced it "good" two times, a double portion for the Teacher.

On this third day, generations appeared. God filled the earth with beautiful, bountiful vegetation, and within each plant He placed the ability to reproduce. This reproductive ability reflects the Teacher's great capacity to bless generations, in his own family and in the families of others. What an awesome responsibility and privilege!

Truth is the playing field and the plumb line for the Teacher. Truth is like the seed. What a joy and honor for the Teacher to see the seed of truth planted deeply into the hearts of others and then to see it begin to grow and produce fruit in their lives.

And the green plants? Wheat for bread, broccoli for vitamins, and herbs for taste and healing were all present on the third day. The Teacher has the capacity to take grains of truth, to ponder, research, and then release them to the Church as the bread of life. Truth feeds the spirit as the vegetables feed the body, and truth brings healing just as the herbs bring healing.

Slow-growing trees are quite passive. Although nothing seems to be happening, the tree is absorbing nutrients from the soil, processing the minerals, and preparing the branch for fruit. Suddenly, there is a bud, next a blossom, and then the apple appears.

Recognizing, researching, validating, and documenting truth takes time. While this appears to some as passivity, with nothing happening, we know the Teacher is pondering, documenting, and preparing a nugget of truth that could change a life or shift a nation.

Drawn by the wisdom and long-suffering of the Teacher, the broken and wounded feel safe in his presence. His ever-ready ear listens to those around him, and his heart releases words of wisdom, binding up wounds and healing the sick.

Jehovah-Nissi

Exodus 17:8. Jehovah-Nissi. Our standard. Our victory. The battle with the Amalekites was quite the game changer for the nation of Israel. Until this battle, they had functioned as slaves. But on this day they began to see themselves as Jehovah saw them: the sons of Israel, a nation set apart for Himself. No longer passive slaves, on this day they would acknowledge themselves as His sons.

There is a huge difference between a slave and a son. The slave makes no decisions for himself, and his master provides all his needs. If he doesn't have it, he doesn't need it. Even if the obedient slave is well-treated and loved, he does not share in the father's estate. Neither does he own any property, including his own life.

A son, on the other hand, has relationship with his father, gets his identity from his father, and takes responsibility for his father's property.

Until this battle, the nation of Israel had expected Moses and his rod to meet all of their needs. This was rather like being a slave in Egypt. In Egypt, the rod of Moses turned the water to blood and brought the flies, frogs, and other plagues. When they needed deliverance at the Red Sea, Moses' rod parted the sea, and they crossed over on dry ground. When they needed anything at all, they looked to Moses' rod for their provision.

Since they saw themselves as slaves, the predatory Amalekites also saw them this way and attacked to enslave them again. The Israelites' first inclination was to look to the rod of Moses for deliverance. After all, that is what slaves do. Assuming no responsibility, the people would passively wait for the Lord and Moses to take care of any problem they might encounter.

Ah! But this day was different. Moses called the people together and brought Joshua up front. The Lord had promised to be their God

The Gift of Teacher

and their Father, but if they were to be his sons, they would need to take responsibility and actually fight in a battle led by Joshua.

What? Where was Moses' rod? You know—the one with the power, the one that parts the seas and defeats enemies? Can you imagine their questions?

No rod of deliverance today. This day they would strap on a sword and fight. Were they a little anxious? Probably so. They had never actually fought in a battle. But they could see the fire by night and the cloud by day. They had come to recognize this Presence that was alive, powerful, and stayed with them constantly.

Did they trust Joshua and Moses? Yes.

Would the Lord go with them? Yes.

Would he show His supernatural presence as at the Red Sea? Yes.

Determined, they rose up that day, ready to fight.

This battle took place before the day of cell phones and walkie-talkies. The only reliable communication would have been with banners. Each family unit, each group unit, each tribe, and each group of tribes had a banner. The Tabernacle itself was called the Covenant Banner. By looking at the banners, Israel's military positions could readily be identified.

The Israelites had seen other nations' banners and were aware that each banner represented a specific king. But Israel's banner was not a woven piece of cloth. Their banner was the living fire by night and cloud by day that covered their nation.

Historically, when experienced armies defeated their foe, they would tear the banners of the enemy into shreds and tie these shreds onto their own banners. In the heat of battle, the weary warrior could look to the shreds on his banner, remember past victories, and gain courage to fight until another victory came.

Just before the battle with the Amalekites, Moses went up on the mountain so that this inexperienced ragtag slave army could see him. He lifted his rod up to the heavens, thus reminding the Israelites that their banner was the Living God of heaven.

As the warriors saw his rod lifted high, it was as if God Himself was reminding them of their past victories. Remember the Red Sea. Remember the plagues of Egypt. Remember, I AM your God. I AM the God of the cloud by day and the fire by night. I AM the God of Abraham, Isaac, and Jacob. I AM Jehovah, the Supreme Ruler of the Universe, and I AM Nissi, your Banner. I AM!

Yesterday they were a ragtag group of slaves. Yesterday they took no responsibility for themselves. But today they would move from slavery to sonship. Today they would shift from no inheritance to full inheritance. Today they would rise up in maturity and leadership and actively take responsibility for themselves and their nation.

I wonder as they ran to the battle, with fire coursing through their veins, did they feel the shift? The night before, they may have had many doubts and fears, but today they could smell the scent of victory.

As they fought throughout the day, Moses continued to hold up his rod, the reminder of the authority and power of their God, the God of cloud and fire.

However, as the day began to fade and the arms of Moses grew heavy, the battle still raged on. When his arms came down, the Israelites began to lose the fight. Would the assured victory of the morning end in defeat tonight? Suddenly, Hur and Aaron were there by Moses' side. Taking his arms, they lifted the rod of God high. Leading the troops in the valley below, Joshua began to shout, "Look up! Fight on!" Rallying each other with shouts of "Remember the Red Sea!" and "Remember the plagues!" these passive, unseasoned warriors began to fight as sons. Sons of the God of the cloud and fire. Sons of Jehovah-Nissi. As this fresh wind of encouragement swept across the battlefield, the victory was theirs. Theirs to celebrate, theirs to relish. Theirs to tell their children in the days to come.

Teacher, there is a time to remain quiet, only watching, listening, pondering, and being passive. But there comes a time to fight. There is a time to wait, but there is a time to run into the fray. Is it difficult to shift from passivity to confrontation? Yes. Is it necessary? Yes. But know this, Teacher, when you arise to confront, the results are spectacular!

At this battle and shortly thereafter, a paradigm shift occurred in two arenas. By active participation, the slaves became sons, and the government of the nation shifted.

The Israelites' perception of their God and themselves changed. Jehovah required them to be proactive, to be confrontational, and to participate in the battle. Because of this, the Israelites could count on His presence for the victory. They "got it!" He was their God, and they were his sons. They saw themselves as He saw them. His people. His nation. His sons.

But more took place than the victory in the valley. Aaron and Hur had stepped up to the plate during the battle and were now ready for more responsibility in the camp. Moses began to recognize maturity, leadership ability, and a new level of trustworthiness in the people. Trusting the people with increased authority, a new governmental system was established by Moses upon the advice of his father-in-law, Jethro.

Exodus 18:20-21. "And you shall teach them the statutes and the laws, and show them the way in which they must walk and the work they must do. Moreover you shall select from all the people able men, such as fear God, men of truth, hating covetousness; and place such over them to be rulers of thousands, rulers of hundreds, rulers of fifties, and rulers of tens."

Now these passive slaves had become responsible governmental leaders. Moses appointed judges among the people because he was willing to share the burden of leadership with these reliable, dependable sons of God.

Once again, we see the double blessing of the Teacher gift in this portion. We see the shift from passive slaves to proactive sons and a governmental shift for the nation.

The Showbread and the Priesthood

In the Tabernacle, as the priest left the Brazen Altar and cleansed himself at the Bronze Laver, he moved into the Holy Place, which was the inner court. Here there were three pieces of furniture: the Table of Showbread, the Menorah with seven lights, and the Table of Incense.

The two components in the Tabernacle that correspond to the Teacher's double portion are the Table of Showbread and the Priest. In fact, the entire Priesthood as a whole, their duties, responsibilities and position.

First, let's get a picture of the priesthood as it reflects the Teacher gift. The tribe of Levi as a whole was Teacher gift. The Levites had no allotted portion in the nation. Although Jehovah's heart was to dwell among His people, because of their sin He could not, but His representatives could. These Levite families were to reside among all of the tribes to set the plumb line of truth or standard of living for the nation, and to be available to the people throughout the year for healing, pronouncing judgments, and releasing blessings, particularly Aaron's Blessing.

The position of the priesthood in its entirety represented the Teacher gift in the Tabernacle. As a whole, the priests were busy people, killing and burning the sacrifices, inspecting for diseases, pronouncing healing, and blessing the people. After these duties, a priest would move to the laver for cleansing and then move into the Holy Place. While there, he would keep the Menorah lit, partake from the table of Showbread, and burn the incense as a sweet smelling fragrance to the Lord. Once a year, he took the blood of the Lamb behind the veil into the Holy of Holies.

There were strict requirements of maintenance for all the furniture in the Tabernacle. The holy fire at the Brazen Altar must be kept kindled and the water in the laver always fresh. The Showbread, the Menorah, the incense, and the veil at the Holy of Holies each required the priests' attention. As the priest went about these duties, he kept the standard of holiness or true worship in the Tabernacle, never skipping any step nor taking his duties for granted.

The grace gift of Teacher is charged with the responsibility of keeping the standard of true worship and the truth of the spoken word upheld as the Church gathers together to worship. In his quest for truth the Teacher does not want to skip any portion of validation for fear he might miss an important element, thus negating the whole. Therefore, their validation is extremely essential, because it is this standard, required by the Lord, which brings freedom to others. Jesus said in John 8:32, "You shall know the truth, and the truth shall make you free."

Yet, teacher, in your busyness of constantly validating the truth you can become so enamored with the process you can miss the weightiness of the Truth Himself. You can be caught up in the urgent and neglect the important. Activity without relationship empowers a religious spirit.

Just as the priests were given the responsibility of releasing wise counsel, healing, and blessing, yet did not go out and bring people into the tabernacle, so the passive teacher, also designed with this same anointing, waits for others to seek him out.

The second part of the double portion in the Tabernacle was the Showbread. Twelve loaves were set on a table of gold, representing the government of God. Numbers in the Bible have specific meanings. The number 12 represents government. Recognizing Jehovah as Sovereign King and Ruler of the Universe was the governmental position of the priest. God designed the Teacher, like Daniel, to decree His government in the earth. However, this is possible only to the degree that the Teacher intimately knows Him.

One of the ways this intimacy would come for the priest was through the partaking of the Showbread, called the Bread of His Presence or the Bread of His Face. Because it was unleavened, it had to be pierced to keep air from forming bubbles in the dough while it baked. When the priest peered into this round loaf of bread, tradition says he could see the face of God. What an awesome privilege to go into this Holy Place and look into the face of God, physically partaking of His presence, much as we do at our communion table. In eating this most holy bread, the priest was given the ultimate opportunity to experience the manifest presence of Jehovah.

The second portion for the priest, following His time of ministry inside the Tabernacle, was to come out and release Aaron's blessing to the people. Now, with great confidence he could release the blessing of Jehovah's shining face to the people because he had gazed into that very face in the Tabernacle. And from this position he could release the righteous and just judgments of Jehovah's government in the earth.

Thus he fulfilled the two great commandments: To love God and to love men.

While the Teacher intensely desires, searches for, and devours truth, the Lord presents him with the same weighty opportunity. Like the priest, the Teacher is called to spend time in God's presence, gazing at His face. Never being satisfied with simply knowing the truth, he must intentionally seek the face of the God of Truth. But like the priest, the Teacher could allow the busyness of ministry to rob him of the most sacred part of his call—experiencing His presence, seeing His face. Without this relationship with the Father, the activity of religion and the busyness of the work of ministry empower and activate a religious spirit. Truth without His presence becomes legalistic and kills. Jesus said the letter of the law brings death, but the spirit of the law brings life.

The Table of Incense, representing worship, was positioned behind the Table of Showbread, implying that truth must come before worship. This order keeps us doctrinally sound, grounding us and allowing our worship to go deeper. Truth with intimacy is the plumb line of worship. Jesus said we must worship in spirit and in truth. Sometimes in our churches, for example, some of the songs we sing are not doctrinally sound. Recognizing this, the Teacher can bring correction, keeping the plumb line of truth in worship. When we assemble as the Church, the grace gift of Teacher is essential for keeping our gatherings grounded in truth but open to His manifest presence.

Teacher Stronghold and Root Iniquity: A Religious Spirit and Selective Responsibility

Activity without relationship empowers a religious spirit. The Teacher can look very busy. He studies the Word, quotes the Word easily, and is usually doctrinally sound. However, without the Spirit of God permeating his life, he becomes as a sounding brass or a tinkling cymbal. In other words, dead works.

The Teacher is called to embrace and live out both the first and the second commandment. It is difficult to love God with all of one's heart, soul, mind, and strength without loving one's neighbor. Jesus called the religious leaders of His day to task about their lack of concern for others. He rebuked them for keeping the law but neglecting to care for their parents. They looked great on the outside but lived in legalism, instructing others to carry burdens under the law that they themselves could not carry. In Matthew 23:27-29, Jesus called the scribes and Pharisees whitewashed tombs full of dead men's bones. Outwardly, they appeared righteous, but inside they were lawless hypocrites. The Pharisees knew and kept the letter of the law, but in their attempt to impose it on others, they became captive to a religious spirit.

When fully convinced of a truth, the Teacher will be like a dog with a bone. Although this tenacity is a good trait, it can also become a point of pride, opening the door to the same religious spirit manifested as pride. The prideful Teacher closes his ears to other perspectives or opinions of value and breaks relationship over a truth issue. The Bible does say there is wisdom in a multitude of counselors, but if the Teacher only listens to those who agree with him, he is in a precarious position. Being open to the Spirit of the Lord is vital for a Teacher in this position. Like the priest in the Tabernacle, he must know the God of the Word, not just the Word. Staying open to hear the voice of God is the key to this dilemma.

The Teacher gift carries two chains of root iniquity: selective responsibility or denial and an unwillingness to impose responsibility on others.

The Teacher who lives in denial can convince himself he is busy about the Lord's work and, in the frenzy of activity, can choose urgent tasks over his most important responsibility, spending time with the Father. For example, the priest, enveloped in the fragrance of worship from the Table of Incense, would stop at the Table of Showbread. Here, he had the amazing privilege of gazing into the face of the Most High. However, if his heart was not hungry, he could miss the most important portion of his birthright, knowing the Father face to face. Ezekiel 22:24 states, "My priests have not distinguished between the holy and unholy, nor have they made known the difference between the unclean and the clean."

By allowing his duties in the Tabernacle to become routine, even while continuing to perform them to the letter of the law, the priest could unknowingly empower a religious spirit. In addition, his unwillingness to recognize his lack of relationship with God would keep this religious spirit locked in place.

May I remind you here of the definition of iniquity—missing the mark with such prevalence it becomes "normal" to us. The control of a religious spirit, coupled with the root iniquity of denial, begins to feel normal. It will keep the Teacher's destiny chained and hide the treasure within him.

Jesus spoke of a priest in the story of the Good Samaritan. Putting myself in the priest's position, I'm sure his mind was on all he had to accomplish for the day. Perhaps he was wearing beautiful, freshly laundered garments and was running late. He may have had a fleeting thought of helping this poor man. But if he stopped to help him, his robes might get soiled, and his urgent priestly duties might be neglected. Besides, the choice to help might cost him time and money, neither of which he wanted to spend. So he walked on, feeling mighty holy, his religious spirit intact. He took responsibility in some areas, while ignoring the hard choices.

In the case of Nadab and Abihu, found in Leviticus 10, the fire on the sacred altar had become common to them. Because they offered "strange fire," or fire from a source other than what God had ordained, they were killed. Just as the religious spirit killed Nadab and Abihu physically, so it can also kill the Teacher spiritually.

Unwillingness to impose responsibility on others is the second chain that keeps this rich treasure bolted down. Recognizing sin is not difficult for the Teacher, because comprehension of the truth is their strength. However, avoiding confrontation at all costs, he will teach it and teach it in the assembly, expecting a specific sinner to hear it and change his ways. Here the Teacher is reluctant to confront the sinner or to ask him to assume responsibility for his sin. In the same vein, the Teacher balks at the idea of asking an already-busy person to take on any further duties.

It is not enough for the Teacher to be righteous; he must confront and lead, especially in his own family. Confronting and imposing responsibility sanctifies his family and releases the generational blessing intended for them.

This is particularly true for a pastor who is a Teacher. He must teach sound doctrine, willingly confront sin in the camp, and call others to take responsibility, thus releasing the generational blessing God intended for his congregation.

Time with Father

The Teacher must make the hard choices and obey all that the Lord commands. While loving Him with all his heart, soul, mind, and strength, he must also actively love his neighbor. But even this can become religious activity unless the Teacher's life is permeated with the presence of the Living God. Time in the presence of the Father is the only way the Teacher gift can avoid being captured by a religious spirit.

The Teacher has a double anointing to reveal God's manifest Presence through worship in spirit and truth and to legislate the Kingdom of heaven into the earth realm. However, he cannot reveal what he does not carry and cannot legislate a kingdom he does not understand. The only way for the Teacher to be successful in these two areas is to halt religious activity and actively gaze into the Father's face, resting in Him, intimately knowing the God of the Word, not just the Word.

But what happens, Teacher, when you have thoroughly taught the people around you an important issue, and you still see the problem in their lives? You know you must actively address the issue, yet in your passivity you feel paralyzed. What do you do? Do you teach it one more time? Or do you confront—which the situation requires? Can you impose responsibility on others? This is most difficult for you, Teacher, yet your Creator knew this when He created you. You cannot do it, but He did! He made a way for you, the way of the Cross.

Jesus as Teacher

Reflecting the Teacher gift in the earth, Jesus understood the grief of asking others to accept personal responsibility. Yet He willingly invited the rich young ruler to come and join the group, knowing how much it would cost this young man. After the young ruler refused to pay the price to become a disciple, Jesus did not run after him, nor did He change the standard to make it more pleasant for him. He let him go.

Jesus knew the Word well. He had studied Torah and was ready to defeat His enemy with the words, "It is written." He made the hardest choice of all, the choice of the cross. When asked to quote the greatest commandment, He directly confronted the religious spirit as He stated the importance of loving God and loving man.

He was proactive and confrontational as he cleansed the temple of the moneychangers, ate grain and healed on the Sabbath. Since He was safe to be around, the children loved Him and crowds were drawn to Him. Most importantly, He spent time with His Father and knew Him face to face. He told his disciples He had "bread they knew not of," the Bread of His Presence.

Last Words of Jesus on the Cross: "John, behold your mother."

It was Passover, and the High Priest was busy with religious activities to be performed on this high, holy day. Jesus, our High Priest, had much to accomplish also. He was the Lamb, on display at 9:00 a.m. for the world to see. At 3:00 p.m., as the Passover lamb was sacrificed, Jesus our Passover Lamb was sacrificed on a cruel cross. The blood of our Lamb would be placed on an altar in a Tabernacle not made with hands. His holy blood would cover our sin, not just for the year, but for all eternity.

As we watched this drama unfold, we witnessed Him unjustly accused, beaten, mocked, and judged as a thief. We heard Him forgive when there had been no confession of sin. And we stood amazed as He rose up in full authority as the Life-giver, releasing life to a dying man and opening the atmosphere of creation for abundant life. Yet in the middle of all the spiritual activity of saving the world, we now see this Great Teacher look at His family and assume responsibility for His mother.

The law stated if the oldest son died, the second son should assume responsibility for his parent. Our Savior, grace gift Teacher, never assumed anything. He personally stopped in the midst of redeeming the world to take care of His family.

Just as a religious spirit caused the busy priest to pass by on the other side of the road, that same religious spirit could have caused Jesus to be too busy saving the world to notice or take care of His mother. But He stopped, took notice, and did the right thing, not allowing the urgent to usurp the important.

The first time Jesus ministered publicly in the synagogue, He stated that He had come to bind up the brokenhearted. At the cross, many of His followers were confused and disillusioned. Others were sad and disappointed. But the most brokenhearted person at the cross was His mother.

"John, will you take care of My mother?"

Precious words from the precious Son of Mary.

Why John?

Jesus knew that John was a grace gift of Mercy. He knew that the Mercy gift is always drawn to the brokenhearted, and He knew this was the right match. John would instinctively know how to minister to Mary. When Mary needed to talk, John would know. When she needed to sit quietly, he would know that, too. John would be the one to help bind up her broken heart.

Jesus also knew that the newly birthed Church would turn to John for answers and that John would be busy traveling and teaching the thousands of new converts as the Church spread worldwide. Yet, conscious of all the responsibility John would have, He still asked, "John, will you take care of My mother?"

You see, Teacher, the Ancient of Days Himself saw your dilemma; He saw your active life. He saw both your grief as confrontation becomes unavoidable and your paralysis as you attempt to impose responsibility on others. In His kindness and love, He did it for you.

Perhaps there is more to this story. As I studied this, I wondered, "Why John? Why not Jesus' brother James, who was the obvious choice to take care of Mary. Why not Matthew?" Here is my conclusion, and it is strictly my thought.

"John, take care of My Mother."

Could it be that the compassion and love of Jesus for His mother was so great He wanted to make sure all of the stored memories and treasures in her heart would be heard and honored? Could it be He

The Gift of Teacher

knew that of all the gifts, the Mercy gift of John would spend the time to hear the heart of Mary? Was it essential that the world know His mother's perspective on His birth, life, and resurrection? I believe He thought so. She had pondered, meditated on, and treasured memories for thirty-three years. She was a rich source of information and revelation about her Son. She knew what the angel of the Lord said to her when she agreed to carry the Son of God in her womb. She now understood the prophecy of Simeon at the temple. Oh yes! John would plumb the depths of her heart for the wisdom from this Teacher gift, Mary, the mother of Jesus.

If anyone really knew who He was, it was Mary. She knew that He was more than a baby born in a cave. She knew that He was with God in the beginning and He was God. He was the Word incarnate. And she knew He came into the world, but the world didn't recognize Him.

The synergy between the Mercy gift and the Teacher gift is amazing. The Teacher's persistence in holding to the truth above all else is essential to keep the Mercy grounded. And the ability to see beyond and know there is more can help the teacher look up from their research and experience His glory in new ways.

The other writers seem to 'stick to the facts' in their account of the birth of Jesus, but not John, the Mercy. In His time with Mary, as he listened to her account of how the supernatural coincided with the natural, he saw beyond the facts and grasped the infinite knowledge of who Jesus REALLY is.

John's account says it this way: John 1:1-5. "In the beginning was the Word, and the Word was with God, and the Word was God. [2]He was in the beginning with God. [3]All things were made through Him, and without Him nothing was made that was made. [4]In Him was life, and the life was the light of men. [5]And the light shines in the darkness, and the darkness did not comprehend it."

A collaboration of both a Mercy and a Teacher who knew Him intimately? Maybe. Just my thoughts.

The Treasure of the Teacher

The ultimate goal of digging for truth is to gather knowledge, reveal the Kingship of Jesus, and respond to that revelation in high, holy worship. Teacher, you fulfill your design when you step out in responsibility and launch into governing from the heavenly realm. As your worship penetrates into the throne room, you see heaven's strategy and declare the government of God into the earth as Daniel did.

The herbs in the garden were for healing. The people came to the priests for healing. Imparting God's wisdom and authority for healing spirit, soul, and body, you carry a rich anointing for healing.

Bringing the plumb line of truth into worship, authority rests with you to tear down the religious spirit as you actively pursue His presence.

One of your greatest joys is to plant the truth in good soil. As you sow truth lavishly into the lives of all you meet, God will bring those specific ones for you to mentor and guide. Your patience, counsel, and even pruning will release generational blessings into their lives and assist them to come into their destiny.

We need you, Teacher. Bring your wisdom, true worship, and double portion anointing to merge synergistically with those around you, releasing yet another blend of His glorious light.

Chapter Five
The Gift of Exhorter

Wonderful, exciting, noisy, glitzy Exhorter! You have twice as many words as all the other gifts and are able to move large numbers of people, spiritually and physically. You are God's world changer. You are a party looking for a place to happen. Everybody loves the Exhorter, and he loves everybody.

Drawing others quickly to himself, readily opening their hearts to his message, he has thousands, millions, maybe gazillions of words. But the question is, "What message does he implant into those hungry hearts?" Does he reveal the spectacular Great God of the Universe?

Exhorter Characteristics

- "Presentation" describes the Exhorter gift. Horizontal in relationships, the exhorter loves people and people love him. Whether it is a party, a speech, or the Gospel, no one presents like the Exhorter. His timing is **exemplary** in his ability to "hit the punch line" just right.

- Very relational and a master communicator, the high profile Exhorter mobilizes masses of people. He is God's world changer.

- He enjoys reading what the Teacher has validated, although he doesn't care to do the deep research. As he presents this truth to the Church with great light and revelation, his teaching significantly moves the hearts of people.

- The Exhorter is able to see root problems, visualize steps of action, and raise hope for solutions. Thus, many are willing to listen to what he has to say.

- He easily crosses socio-economic, political, and racial barriers and is capable of having significant disagreements without breaking fellowship. The flexible Exhorter brings balance and reconciliation at a high level. He makes an excellent statesman.

- New ideas and truth do not intimidate him. He is quick to see opportunities and to take advantage of the momentum. Sometimes setting unrealistic goals, he may start a project prematurely and will quickly abandon it if he sees it is not working.

- He is not quick to accept the supernatural. His motto is "Show me." He needs proof to believe.

- Usually the center of attention, dramatic, and fun to be around, the Exhorter draws people to himself. This is good because he does not relish being alone.

- Most Exhorters love "bling" and colors. Female exhorters seem to instinctively know how to put that extra flourish to any outfit, table setting, or other presentation. When teaching, I usually check out the ladies' shoes. An easy way to spot a Prophet is her shoes are usually designed and compliment the outfit, sharp but not flashy. An easy way to spot an Exhorter—look for the "bling" or bright colors. Once, in a meeting, I had pegged a woman as a Prophet. She wore a tailored black outfit, and her makeup and hair were perfect. She was very good looking and had it together. As I began teaching on the Exhorter, she smiled and slowly slipped her foot out into the aisle. Bling! She wore bright red five-inch heels. Definitely an Exhorter.

- Exhorters love to extend friendships horizontally with people. However, they can become addicted to their smiling faces and find it difficult to go against public opinion. In this case, they will avoid confrontation with these people at all costs.

- The carnal Exhorter never wants to be uncomfortable. Because he is unwilling to make hard choices, he will compromise to get what he wants. This vacillation opens the door to a Jezebel spirit who says, "You don't have to pay full price! I can get it for you the cheaper, easier way."

- He has a tendency to keep others waiting, to look to himself for solutions, and to treat others as projects. He can give up on uncooperative people. Operating "in the nick of time," he waits until the last minute to get things done.

- Because the Exhorter can bring hope and move masses of people, the enemy targets him with discouragement.

- Always wanting to be with others, he is called to spend time alone with the Lord. Think about Moses on the backside of the desert and Paul in the Arabian Desert or years in prison. It is in the "alone place" where the Exhorter learns to go vertically deep with God rather than staying horizontally broad with people.

Exhorter Characteristics as Seen in Bible Personalities

Moses, nation mover; Jeremiah, very dramatic prophet; Saul, the first king of Israel; and Paul, great evangelist, all appeared to be exhorters. Our study will be about Moses.

Moses

Facing death as an infant, Moses was raised in a king's palace and lived in a desert. He experienced a burning bush, a burning mountain, and a parted sea. It doesn't get more dramatic than the life of Moses. Third children share many of the same character qualities as the Exhorter. Moses, a third child and an Exhorter, had a double portion of many of these character qualities, rather like an Exhorter on steroids.

Being raised in the palace of Pharaoh, I am sure Moses had his share of elaborate trappings, throngs of adoring fans, and lots of "bling." But this was not enough for Moses. Knowing he was a Hebrew and desiring to go broader, he wanted the approval of the tribes of Israel as well. In an effort to win their favor, he killed an Egyptian. Can we say compromise of standards resulted in a quick exit to the desert shortly after the murder?

When the Exhorter is up, he is up, but when he is down, he is way down. We next find our mighty Exhorter Moses on the backside of the Sinai Desert tending sheep, far away from the adoring crowds.

We have read the books and seen the movies of his encounter with God, but let's look a little deeper. Moses the Exhorter craved to be with people but spent 40 years in this lonely place. Back in Egypt, he experienced a life of great honor and advantage. Did he miss the splendor of that lifestyle and the favor and patronage of the Pharaoh? Now the "bling" was gone, the desert was hot, and he wore the homespun clothes of a shepherd. Pretty tough circumstances for an Exhorter who loves people and the comfort of the "good life!"

Quite possibly, his Hebrew mother had told Moses the remarkable story of his birth. She may have impressed upon him that God had a purpose and a destiny for him. Remembering those conversations in this lonely time of life, his thoughts were probably, "Yeah? Right."

Stripped of his former glory, his hope gone for the "big destiny and purpose," it seemed as though Moses would live out the rest of his life here in the Sinai, tending his father-in-law's sheep. Resigned to this humble lifestyle, Moses was finally ready for the most dramatic encounter of his life—the game changer—a face-to-face meeting with the Ancient of Days Himself.

One day Moses stepped aside to watch a dry bush spontaneously burn. Following this phenomenal encounter, Moses was sent back to Egypt. Not as the disgraced prince of Egypt, but as the ambassador of the King of the Universe. He was not dressed extravagantly in the superficial display of Egypt, but he was clothed in the power and authority of the Great Jehovah. He walked not with a scepter of gold, but with a stick. Yep, just a stick, but what a stick! It was the rod of God Himself.

Moses moved from using his natural abilities and desires, as wonderful as they were, into flowing in the supernatural anointing of his DNA, his grace gift. God pulled him away from the party, away from the approval of Egypt, away from the comfort and the easy way of having every desire met into His greater plan for Moses. That plan was his birthright. These 40 years alone with God, being stripped of the allure of fame and position and broken by the loss of his visions of grandeur, shifted Moses into his greatest anointing, his supernatural destiny. This anointing did not come cheap or easy, but it was worth the high price.

Designed by his Creator to be the life of the party, to love the dramatic, and to move masses of people, Moses' blueprint did not change. God simply shifted Moses to the right party, with the right people and the right presentation.

The fame of Moses became greater, his place of authority larger, and the dramatic, well, let's just say, he advanced from burning bushes to burning mountains, from smiling faces of people to the brilliant countenance of Jehovah. He was forever spoiled for anything Egypt had to offer.

This great Exhorter, functioning at the highest level of his design, was truly a world changer and a reconciler. He moved a nation of people from one location to another, from a natural kingdom to a holy kingdom of priests, and from slavery into sonship. An entire nation was reconciled back to God.

Exhorter's Foundational Principle: Sowing and Reaping

The Exhorter's foundational principle is sowing in season to reap a harvest in due time. A mature Exhorter's anointing for discerning times and seasons, both in the spiritual and natural realm, is amazing.

Sowing and reaping take time. For the excited, impatient Exhorter, it is imperative he understand the importance of waiting. Planting an apple tree today does not produce apple pies tomorrow. Enjoying the present and always being willing to sow seeds of hope and vision, it is often painful to wait for those seeds to germinate, to grow, and to produce fruit. Maturity calls for him to embrace the pain of waiting and watching, watering and fertilizing, before the harvest is ready to reap. And, most often, the Lord requires him to wait alone.

Exhorter's Birthright: To Know God Face to Face

The birthright of the Exhorter is to know our glorious God face to face and to see His knowledge, character, and wisdom revealed in the season in which he is living. He cannot give away what he does not own. Going deep with God and paying the price to know Him face to face give the Exhorter a key to an understanding of God that releases all the other gifts. His ability to build relationships across all boundaries and understand times and seasons positions the wise Exhorter to bring light and revelation to masses. From this position, he can influence large groups of people toward reconciliation with God and each other, and even shift nations.

Living in the fullness of his birthright requires embracing the pain of personal discomfort and the agony of waiting. This gives him the strength and wisdom to resist compromise and release the peace of Jehovah-Shalom.

Fourth Day of Creation

Genesis 1:14-19. "Then God said, 'Let there be lights in the firmament of the heavens to divide the day from the night; and let them be for signs and seasons, and for days and years; and let them be for lights in the firmament of the heavens to give light on the earth'; and it was so. Then God made two great lights: the greater light to rule the day, and the lesser light to rule the night. He made the stars also. God set them in the firmament of the heavens to give light on the earth, and to rule over the day and over the night, and to divide the light from the darkness. And God saw that it was good. So the evening and the morning were the fourth day."

On the fourth day, the firmament exploded with marvelous, spectacular lights as the sun, moon, and stars appeared. It was noisy in space. Job proclaimed the morning stars sang as God flung them out. Shining on all creation, these lights continue to declare His glory, govern times and seasons, and divide the darkness. Stars are used for navigational purposes, and they were even used to announce the Savior's birth.

Scientists tell us the universe is ever expanding. New stars are being birthed every day as our Creator God extends His glory and majesty in the stars.

Our whole planetary system, our planet, and even our lives are governed through proximity and relationship.

The moon governs the tides through relationship. The proximity of the moon to the earth creates a magnetic pull, causing the tides to rise and fall and move great masses of water twice a day. Although we use the Roman solar calendar, the Biblical calendar is set to the timing of the moon. In Genesis, the new day begins at sundown. "It was evening and morning, the first day." The Jewish people use sundown as the precise time in the evening to begin their holy days and Sabbaths. The new moon rising designated the first day of each month and the beginning of the monthly First Fruits celebration called Rosh Chodesh.

According to the Roman calendar, the sun governs our times and seasons. When the sun is straight overhead, we say it is 12 o'clock noon. We rise, sleep, and plan our activities around the sun, which dictates our seasons, sheds light and heat on our planet, and determines our planting and harvest cycles.

The correlation between the Exhorter and these two heavenly bodies is easily seen in governing through relationship. Everyone loves to be around the Exhorter. He is usually in the center, and others revolve around him. His ability to gather people, to bring unity, and to move hearts is unprecedented. He accomplishes his purposes and gets things done through relationships. When used incorrectly, we might call this manipulation. However, if his heart is pure, the Lord can use his potential and skills to transform cities and nations.

Like the sons of Issachar who understood the times and seasons and knew what to do in them, the Exhorter is ordained to have dominion over time. The tendency of the Exhorter to move "in the nick of time" is not God's best plan for him. Intending him to govern time, not vice versa, God designed him to know, value, and appropriate time and to be instinctively aware of when to wait and when to shift. The Exhorter has the ability to establish God's time in the earth. He may never have a more orderly time schedule, but he is the key to timing.

Everything in creation has limits except the stars. I recommend you go to the Hubble Telescope website. Look and listen to the awe-inspiring sights and sounds of the planets and stars. View the spectacular galaxies and experience the wonder of deep space. The blend of the sounds coming out of these giants of light will astonish and amaze you.

The Exhorter is known for his exuberance, his excitement, and his multitude of words. God made Exhorters to pour forth speech, declare His glory, and proclaim His magnificence and His greatness just like the stars.

Seen as jewels in the sky, each star is unique with a distinct light and sound all its own. Drawing from the deep research of the Teacher, the Exhorter discovers the unlimited jewels in scripture and sheds fresh light on the same passage. In so doing, he causes crisp, refreshing revelation to burst forth like these brilliant diamonds in the nighttime sky.

It is not the quantity but the quality of the message of the Exhorter that is pertinent. By welcoming rather than chafing at time spent alone and by intimately seeking God's presence and His face, the Exhorter's relationship with God will grow deeper. This deepened relationship will cause his horizontal relationships to increase in wisdom, discernment, and influence. The only limit for the Exhorter is speaking of matters too small. I saw a poster once that said, "It is not that I exaggerate the facts, I just remember bigger." God designed the Exhorter to see and speak of bigger matters.

Although he should never compromise the truth by false exaggeration, neither should he limit his message to men's wisdom. God's wisdom is without limits just like our universe. As he intentionally deepens his relationship with God by studying His character, the Lord will intentionally increase his influence and wisdom horizontally. The magnitude of proclamation and declaration of God's glory is His design and purpose for the Exhorter. My prayer for the Exhorter is he will be remembered for the quality of his message, not by how many words it took to say it.

Jehovah-Shalom

Jehovah-Shalom, God is Peace! All the definitions of peace in our dictionary begin with "free from…." Free from disturbance, free from war, free from stress and anxiety, and free from trouble.

Shalom, God's peace, is much more than just being free from chaos. The Hebrew word means full restoration to God's original intent. It is not simply a lack of disturbance, but it is to be put back in order by being filled to overflowing with His comfort, prosperity, and restitution. Nothing missing. Nothing broken.

The compound name of Jehovah-Shalom was given to Gideon in Judges 6. The pivotal question for Gideon was "Can I trust You when there is no evidence of Your presence?"

At this time in Israel's history, their disobedience had opened the door for the Midianites, the Amalekites, and the people of the East to traumatize the nation. The Midianites formed a coalition with the Amalekites and other eastern peoples. The Midianites were descendants of Midian, a son of Abraham and Keturah after Sarah's death. Abraham had given them gifts, but no inheritance. The Amalekites descended from Esau's grandson, Amalek. These enemies were after more than the grain; they were coming to get what they deemed as their inheritance.

These enemies had established a pattern. Each year for seven years, they had withdrawn their armies so the Israelites could plow and plant their fields. At harvest, they would return with their hordes to steal the ripened grain. The Israelites worked hard throughout the planting season but were never allowed the joy and celebration of harvest. They experienced plowing and planting but not harvesting. After seven years, this was getting a little old. The Israelites were hiding in holes and caves just to survive. It was quite evident to everyone that Jehovah had forsaken them. There was no evidence anywhere that He still heard their prayers.

Our story begins with Gideon being visited by the Angel of the Lord as he hid in a wine press. The Angel showed up and declared, "Hello, mighty man of valor!" Shocked, Gideon looked around to discover a stranger standing there speaking to him.

The Gift of Exhorter

Suppose the conversation went like this:

Angel: "Hey, big guy, mighty warrior, great man of courage, I've got a message for you. You can stop hiding, because the Midianites won't be getting your grain this year."

Gideon: "What? Who are you talking to? They come every year. We've cried out to our God, but obviously He isn't listening. So why should this year be any different?"

Angel: "Well, it will be different because you, fierce fighting machine, are going to defeat them and run them off."

Gideon: "Give me a break! I'm from the smallest tribe and the smallest family in Israel. And if I were such a warrior as you seem to think, why would I be hiding in this wine press hole trying to thresh my wheat?"

Angel: "Well, you see, Gideon, I'm a messenger from Jehovah. He has heard your cry and sent me to tell you that you are the man He has chosen for the job. But you don't have to do it alone. Actually, He's going to do the fighting for you, but He's looking for a partner, and you are the man! You're the one He has chosen."

Gideon: "But I didn't apply for that job. In fact, how do I know you aren't just some crazy guy trying to trick me? Can you do something supernatural so I'll know it's you?"

Angel: "Sure, be glad to. Bring me some meat and unleavened bread and put it on this rock."

So Gideon did it, and the Angel touched it with his staff and boom! It burned up! And the angel disappeared.

Gideon: "Great. Now I've done it. Now I'm gonna die."

Gideon knew the stories about what happens when you see God's face. You die.

Believing it's all over, he says, "Man! What was I thinking? And what was that all about anyway?"

Then the voice of the Lord God Jehovah speaks, "Peace be with you; do not fear, you shall not die."

So Gideon built an altar there to the Lord and called it Jehovah-Shalom, The Lord Is Peace.

Shalom. Peace. Jehovah, the Self-existent One, the mighty Sovereign Ruler of the Universe has spoken His Shalom, His full restoration, and all things are put back in order. The God of all comfort would comfort Israel.

The name, Jehovah-Shalom, was given before Gideon's mighty feat of tearing down the Baal altar or leading the army. Representing more than just taking care of Israel's enemies, this name spoke volumes to Gideon. It gave him courage to become who Jehovah saw him to be and gave him the faith to go to battle with only 300 men, flash lights, and clay jars. When there was no evidence of His presence, Jehovah-Shalom spoke, and everything shifted. There was full restoration. Nothing missing. Nothing broken.

In the life of the Exhorter, there are times when Jehovah-Shalom withdraws His tangible presence, leaving no evidence that He is on the scene. Friends, who the Exhorter has relied on walk away and he finds himself in a desert, prison, wine press, or cave. Just as Moses was pulled away from the adoring crowds of Egypt, so the Exhorter is left with nothing and no one to validate that God is still there. Can you trust God's character when you cannot see His face?

During this time, as the Exhorter grasps the significance of his circumstance, he has the opportunity to go vertical with the Lord. Delving deep into the aspects of His character, he begins to see who God really is and His faithfulness. When a covenant-keeping God says, "I will never leave you," He means it. In this place God reveals the blessing of His face to him.

Aaron's blessing states in Numbers 6:24-26, "The Lord bless you and keep you. The Lord make His face shine upon you and be gracious to you. The Lord lift up His countenance upon you and give you peace." Jehovah-Shalom.

When all is devastation around the Exhorter, if he can remember his time in the desert and the character of Jehovah-Shalom, he can make it through the dark times. God's name brings the assurance that His face will surely shine upon him once again. As a covenant-keeping God, He has given his covenant blessing of Shalom, full restoration and full restitution. He has given His covenant word, "I will never leave nor forsake you." Therefore, when all is dark, and there is no evidence He is present, the Exhorter can stand on His unchanging character and believe His word. His face will shine upon you.

The Menorah

There were heavy curtains around and over the inner portion of the Tabernacle. Very little natural light could be seen there. The Golden Lampstand with its seven lights illuminated this room. This light was maintained with pure olive oil. It shed extraordinary light on the priest, the Table of Showbread, and the Table of Incense. There were precise instructions given for making this beautiful lamp made from pure gold and the oil that would be used in it. The seven lights on this lampstand, also called the Menorah, represented the seven-fold Spirit of God found in the books of Isaiah and Revelation.

Just as this lampstand shed light on the Showbread and the Table of Incense, so the Exhorter shines revelatory light on the research of the Teacher and extends the influence of worship horizontally.

A lovely thing to behold, the Menorah is not really the issue here for the Exhorter. We've discussed the light he releases as we talked about the sun, moon, and stars. In the Tabernacle, it is the purity of the oil that becomes the consideration.

This oil had to be pure. It was meticulously prepared according to specific instructions given to Moses. The ingredients for the oil came from the Galilee region of Israel. I believe it is significant that this was also the region where Jesus, the Light of the world, spent much of His time as a boy and as a man near the Sea of Galilee.

The Festival of Lights, or Hanukkah, is an eight-day Jewish holiday, which commemorates the rededication of the holy temple in

Jerusalem at the time of the Maccabeus Revolt in the 2nd century BC. This Festival gives more insight concerning the purity of the oil to be used in the golden lampstand. After they had taken back the temple from the Romans, the Maccabees cleansed it and wanted to relight the lamp, but they only had enough oil for one day. It took four days' journey up to the Galilee and four days back to have the exact oil required for this lamp. Because they refused to use unholy oil, they began the eight-day round trip to bring back pure oil. However, they chose to light the lamp anyway with only a one-day supply.

Hanukkah means, "A miracle happened here!" and it did. The one-day supply lasted eight days, and this became an annual Jewish celebration known as the Festival of Lights. Jesus celebrated this festival, which continues today.

The Maccabees could have chosen the available but impure oil, quicker to attain and at a much cheaper price. But they chose the hard way, to wait and trust God for the pure holy oil.

The addictive pull of the approval of man opens the Exhorter to the spirit of Jezebel. Calling him to compromise his values and integrity, this spirit declares, "I can get it for you cheaper. You really don't have to pay full price, there is always an easier way. Why wait?"

Many times the Exhorter begins well, shining pure light on the word of the Teacher and the worship of the Giver. However, if he becomes obsessed and enamored with the admiration of people, he will begin to mix soul and spirit. Rather than receiving and giving revelation from God, he will begin to release his own opinions and thoughts, causing impure light to come forth. The Exhorter has extraordinary access to the light of God. He must stay alert to compromise in order to release light from a pure source. Saying "No" to the cheaper price, the easier way, his high calling is to spend the time, pay the hard price of waiting, thereby revealing a far-reaching, broader understanding of the nature and character of God.

Exhorter Stronghold and Root Iniquity: Cult of Comfort and Denial

Trudging in from her first day of kindergarten, the cute little blonde dropped her new pink and orange backpack at the door, kicked off her sparkly new shoes, and plopped down in the middle of the floor. With her hair bow drooping, she rolled her eyes dramatically and announced, "I've decided to quit school. I am NOT going back! I guess I'll just be a drop out."

"Why, sweetheart, it's only your first day. Don't you think you might give it a couple of days?" her mom asked, smiling.

"Nope!" she declared emphatically. "It's too long, too hard, and too boring!"

Spoken like a true Exhorter.

The cult of comfort, putting immediate pleasure or comfort ahead of the long-term commitment, is the stronghold of the Exhorter. "Easier! Cheaper! Quicker!" is the call of compromise. The enemy whispers, "Try the easy way, skip the hard stuff, and just stay at the party. After all it's all about you."

The Exhorter's unwillingness to leave people, wade through discomfort, and embrace pain keeps this stronghold intact. Seeking to reap where he has not sown and looking for the easy way out, the Exhorter can become a people pleaser. He likes to go with people, have people go with him, and just be with people. He will refuse to confront Jezebel (sin and compromise) for fear of losing the approval of the masses.

Skirting the issues, the Exhorter may move in denial. Refusing to own his own problems and always explaining his "extenuating circumstances," it seems it is always someone else's fault, someone else's responsibility. Unable to face the consequences for his own failures, he continually asks, "Why me? Why is this happening to me?"

The Exhorter can have a wonderful ministry with lots of people, but he will never fully possess his birthright until he controls his time.

There is no shortcut for time to get to know God. But the tyranny of the urgent dictates where he needs to be, why he needs to be there, and allows his schedule to govern his life-flow. His operating "in the nick of time" robs him from the important tasks while he takes care of the urgent ones. Because he is addicted to the approval of people, he will make choices to please the crowd when the honor of the Lord is at stake.

Refusing to embrace the pain of separation from people, live in purity, or pay the full price, the Exhorter loses the supreme privilege of experiencing Jehovah face to face. Without knowing and understanding His character, the Exhorter's many words become as sounding brass or tinkling cymbal. He can open the hearts of the people, but he will have nothing to pour into them.

A good biblical example of this unredeemed nature is King Saul, Exhorter gift. He was told by God to kill all of the Amalekites and their livestock. He captured King Agag alive, and he allowed the people to take the livestock. Note his words to Samuel in 1 Samuel 15:24-26, "Then Saul said to Samuel, 'I have sinned, for I have transgressed the commandment of the Lord and your words, because I feared the people and obeyed their voice. [25]Now therefore, please pardon my sin, and return with me, that I may worship the Lord.' [26]But Samuel said to Saul, 'I will not return with you, for you have rejected the word of the Lord, and the Lord has rejected you from being king over Israel.'"

Could Saul not see his sin? It was not the sin of simple disobedience to one command, but the sin of choosing the approval of the people over honoring the Lord.

Saul still did not get it. Verse 30 states, "Then he said, 'I have sinned; yet honor me now, please, before the elders of my people and before Israel, and return with me, that I may worship the Lord your God.'" This statement revealed Saul's heart. Having just been told that the Lord had forsaken him and he had lost the kingdom, Saul referred to Jehovah as "your God," not "my God." His pride caused him to be more concerned with loosing face with the people than loosing his relationship with Jehovah.

I can hear the echo of Joshua's command, "Choose you this day whom you will serve." There were two choices made that day. Saul chose the people. Consequently, Jehovah chose David to lead Israel.

Time with Father

What is the answer for the wonderful Exhorter? How can he shift from seeking the people's approval he so desperately craves? He must set his face like flint toward the only face where Shalom peace can be found. Numbers 6:24-26. "The Lord bless you and keep you, the Lord make His face shine upon you, and be gracious unto you, the Lord lift up His countenance upon you, and give you peace." Shalom peace. Even if there is no evidence the Father is near, when the Exhorter, the one with the "show me proof to believe" gift, seeks to know His character, he will have assurance of his Father's love and presence.

Moses spent a second 40 years in the wilderness. There he continued to seek Jehovah's face daily in the tent of meeting outside the camp rather than seek the approval of an unbelieving and disobedient nation. Time with the Lord and in His word is the method to develop the message. The many words and the easy relationships are the vehicles through which to deliver the message. The Exhorter must push through pain, set his face like flint, and come away with God.

But what becomes of you, Exhorter, when the crowds are gone, and you find yourself in the wilderness. Yes, the blessing of Aaron states, "And make His face to shine upon you," but what if you can find no evidence of His face anywhere? Nor can you find anyone else's face, for that matter. No evidence to verify God is still present. You are alone. Deserted. Like Gideon, you might ask, "Can I trust you when I cannot see you?" Is it over for you, disappointed, discouraged Exhorter?

No! Jesus, Creator of the sun, moon and stars, and Creator of you, mighty Exhorter, made a way for you.

Jesus as Exhorter

How did Jesus model the grace gift of Exhorter when He lived upon the earth? He declared, "I AM the Light of the World!" And He is. He moved masses of people, crowds followed him, and many He met loved him. Everyone wanted to be His friend.

We read many times how Jesus withdrew and left the party to seek the face of the Father. Early in the morning or late at night, always beholding the face of His Father, He stated, "I only do what I see My Father doing."

Jesus was willing to endure the pain in the wilderness when he spent forty days without water or food. At his weakest moment, the Prince of Darkness showed up with a compromise. Knowing that Jesus had come for the Kingdom, Satan dangled the keys of the kingdoms in front of him. Offering him the opportunity to get the kingdoms of this world for a cheaper, easier cost, our Champion Jesus chose to see further than His immediate pain. Rising up each time with a ready answer, and looking to the joy set before Him, He defeated Satan with supernatural words from the Old Testament. You see, He was and is the living, breathing Word.

The Last Words of Jesus on the Cross: "My God, My God, why have YOU forsaken me!"

Listening to my son-in-law, Rich Butler, preaching one Sunday, it seemed this portion of the cross opened up to me in a new way. Jesus states in John 16:32-33, "Listen, the hour is coming… that you will be scattered …and will leave me alone. Yet I am not alone, because the Father is with me." Since the beginning, Jesus had never been separated from His Father. The crowds came and went, and even the disciples were not always there for Him. But His Father? He was always near, always communicating, always validating His love for His Son. Jesus understood more completely than anyone else the full measure of Aaron's blessing, the warmth of His Father's face smiling upon Him and keeping Him. His kind eyes, His smiling mouth, even the breath of His nostrils—Jesus knew every detail. He had been on the earth for thirty-three years, talking with Him daily. But long before that, They were One.

"My Father and I are One." Always have been, always will be. For all eternity. Did He long to go back where there was no veil between them?

Now, on the cross, everyone had left, and the Great Darkness was coming upon the earth, the Great Wrath of God. At that moment, Jesus looked up once again to see the nod, the favor, the validation of His Father's face, but it was gone. All He could see was The Darkness. And He was alone. He was ultimately, completely alone.

What went through His mind? His Father, the One with Whom He was so intimately connected, had turned His face away. Instead of His Father's smile, He saw the Darkness, the wickedness, the evil, the chaos. There was no evidence whatsoever that His Father was still present. Only this Great Darkness.

His accuser, this Darkness, had a voice. Rattling the keys of his kingdoms, it hissed, "Remember the wilderness? I would have given you these kingdom keys without all this bloody suffering. It would have been much quicker, much easier. And much less painful."

At that moment, in His most desperate voice, Jesus cried out, "My God! My God! Why have You forsaken me?" You, who called me to this life. You, who called me to this pain, why have You forsaken me?

Jesus had always addressed Him as Abba Father. But this one time, He did not. The word He used for God means supreme, unapproachable magistrate, or judge.

The Supreme Court of the Universe was in session, and the Ancient of Days had taken His seat as judge.

The world was being judged.

What was the penalty to break the curse of the Darkness? Death.

What was the eternal destination of the convicted? Hell.

Who was standing in this eternal courtroom? We were.

At this moment, the Judge of the Universe took this Great Darkness, the entire wrath of the world, and flung it toward us, just as a quarterback throws a football. In His finest hour, our Great Champion, naked, forsaken and despised, reached out with open arms and intercepted this Great Darkness, embracing the wrath, the evil, the chaos, the hell meant for us.

John 3:16-17 (The Message) "This is how much God loved the world: He gave his Son, his one and only Son. And this is why: so that no one need be destroyed; by believing in him, anyone can have a whole and lasting life. God didn't go to all the trouble of sending his Son merely to point an accusing finger, telling the world how bad it was. He came to help, to put the world right again." Jehovah-Shalom. Full restoration.

When He could no longer see His face, Jesus trusted His Father's character. With no evidence anywhere to confirm it, and His enemy whispering in His ear, He still knew and believed: He is good.

Jesus still trusted that Jehovah-Shalom was moving in the earth to restore, rebuild, and renew, because that is His character.

With faith and confidence in His Father's character alone, Jesus intercepted our judgment and continued to endure the torment of the cross because of the joy set before Him. The joy in knowing that now the smile of His Father's face could shine upon you, Exhorter. He had planted the seed in the right season, now He chose to embrace the hard choice, the pain, the judgment, and wait for the harvest. You, Exhorter, are His harvest.

The Treasure of the Exhorter

It is no accident that you are placed smack dab in the middle of the Romans 12 gifts. You are a catalyst for the other gifts to be drawn into your circle of celebration. They all "get along" and reconciliation happens as they see each other in new light (pun intended). Celebrating, reconciling, and just having fun, you are the delight of our Father.

By exploring the depths of His love, you gain the confidence to believe without seeing and encourage others to do so. You are able to teach about His character and speak forth His wisdom to those who gather around you for the party!

Just as the sons of Issachar understood the times and seasons and knew what to do in them, you, mature Exhorter, know when to shift, when to wait, and when to press in for the harvest. While others will always have more orderly schedules, you know how to exercise dominion over time and get the right thing done in the right time. No longer allowing your schedule to dictate your life, your spirit will lead you into God's timing.

The sun and stars are constantly erupting with light. Your highest call is to know God and make Him famous. Your grasp of the revelation of the deep truths discovered by the Teacher helps others visualize and glimpse the magnificence of our remarkable Creator.

Your winning personality, love of people, and abundant, eloquent words position you to present the gospel with such flair that you disarm dissenters, and the world flocks to hear what you have to say. You have a presentation of the Gospel that is second to none. Exhorter, you will be remembered for the magnitude of the message you carry.

Chapter Six
The Gift of Giver

Giver! Some of you are fun, relentless, flexible, an extrovert. Others are life-giving, good listeners, content to remain behind the scenes, an introvert. Difficult to spot, your persistence could identify you as a Prophet or Teacher. At other times you resemble a Mercy, Exhorter, or even a Servant. So who are you really, behind that facade, you chameleon of the grace gifts? You are the "behind the scenes" oil that keeps the body moving forward. Supplies, resources, and networking are your specialties. Being flexible, you seem to find what works and bring that missing piece, the piece others have overlooked. Yes, Giver, you are loved and essential to the Kingdom. Just as the Servant is a "gift" to the Church, even so you are a "treasure."

Giver Characteristics

- The word "value" is important to the Giver. He values quality and appreciates old things, such as antiques because they are well crafted and continue their usefulness into the present day, connecting the past to the present. The Giver also values legacy and wants to provide for future generations, thus connecting the present to the future. Above all, he values individuals across socio-economic, racial, gender, and age boundaries. Recognizing the value of individuals and giving them dignity by pulling them into relationship on even ground with others, he creates community in its highest form.

- Having a broad range of competence and personality characteristics, the Giver is the most diverse and adaptable of the grace gifts. Disliking patterns and seeing outside the box, he will remain open for new ways to accomplish tasks and for innovative ideas.

- God created the Giver to be independent. He never wants to appear needy. He is self-reliant and will look to others for help only as a last resort.

- The Giver is tenacious in his everyday life. He will not give up when convinced what he seeks is correct or necessary. He is relentless until he obtains it. If it is important to the Kingdom of God, then it is important to the redeemed Giver. Like the Giver Jacob in the Bible wrestling the angel, he will not turn loose until he gets what he wants.

- The Giver is like the hub of a wheel, with resources and life flowing out to the Church in unique, assorted ways. He sees resources others miss, and he also sees the value in people that others miss. He makes a place for them to fit in the Church.

- He cherishes freedom of choice and likes to keep his options open so that he can go with the flow, adapt, or change directions in case a better option becomes available. When discussing a plan of action, usually the Giver will be the last one to commit, whether for a vacation, a lunch date, or a mission trip, because a better option might come along. He wants the freedom to make the best choice. What feels like a promise to you is an option to him.

- The flexible Giver does not like patterns, to be predictable or put in a box. If he feels you are expecting something or even demanding a commitment from him, many times he will walk away and leave you with unmet expectations.

- Protective of his assets, the Giver senses hidden agendas, reads the fine print in a contract and hardly ever gives money impulsively. He often finds favor in the eyes of other people concerning money. He moves in supernatural timing, having a keen inner sense of when to invest and when to withhold. He usually does not like to provide for start-up finances, because he wants to make sure his investments are valid and secure. He tends not to invest in the poor, because he has the idea people are poor because they mishandle their funds.

- On the other hand, he can be very generous. When choosing to give, he gives wisely and well. Observing others to discover their preferences, he delights in giving just the right gift to that individual.

- The Giver nurtures his children in a different way than most other gifts. He searches his child's heart to discover the particular quality that needs to be nurtured and valued. Having an eye to the future, he continually prepares him, making sure he learns his lessons well, so his child will thrive as he leaves the nest. Restraining finances insures his child has a good understanding of the value of money, and strong discipline guarantees he is equipped to face life's challenges. To the Giver, his love is very deep and sacrificial. He is willing to exchange his immediate joy of freely giving to his child in order to prepare him for the future. This same Giver can be generous to others, because he does not feel responsible to teach them anything.

- Resources flow easily to him, and he is aware of assets that others often miss. He is able to relate to a wide range of people. Networking comes easily, and he builds community everywhere he goes. Although private in his own life and often secretive about personal details, he loves people and loves to discover facets of their lives that go unnoticed by others.

- These two characteristics seem to work together in unusual ways. I have a friend who is a giver, and I am often amazed at her ability to discover details of strangers' lives within a very short time. After lunch in a new restaurant, I left simply with an opinion about the food. Not my friend. She came away knowing when this restaurant was established, the current owner, the past three owners, why they bought the establishment, where they were from, and even the maiden name of the owner's mother.

- I've observed from being around these gregarious Givers that while these details may seem like useless information to me, these facts are very important to the Giver for two reasons. First, the conversation helps build community and releases life to those to whom they are speaking. After all, who doesn't enjoy talking about himself, especially to someone who is really interested? The second reason is the Giver seems to unconsciously store this information for future use. Later, as a need arises, he can "scan" his information pool and remember if anyone he knows might have a resource that would fit this need. Who knew this "useless" information would be the answer to someone's prayer? Like a PVC conduit pipe, God designed the Giver with unconventional and creative ways to steward His resources.

- Having an immense heart for evangelism, a Giver is often willing to provide supplies to ministries with this focus. Non-confrontational, he will leave the face-to-face witnessing and the spiritual warfare to others, preferring to anonymously furnish the Bibles, buy the gas for the ministers, or support the mission in some other way.

- Always wanting to feel safe and secure on all levels—physical, financial, spiritual, and emotional—is strategic to a Giver. This tendency causes him to be hesitant to make any decision, keeping all his options open to get the best deal or the most secure plan. Because finances and resources flow easily to him, he tends to view his own resources as his security. This need for security can create uncertainty, vulnerability, and fear of not having enough. Falling into a cycle of fear, anxiety, or dread, the Giver may begin to hoard his resources.

- Others often look to the Giver as one who supplies needs in the Church. This might empower a spirit of pride and control, causing the Giver to think he can control others through his resources. Only God can supply all our needs, therefore both the Giver and the recipient are wrong. And if at any time the Giver senses he is seen as the supplier of resources, he will usually leave or withdraw his support.

- The Giver is very intentional with his gifts. He can give with strings attached to make sure the benefits flow back to him and his own best interests. Quickly recognizing when he is being manipulated, he will strongly resist any type of control, even to the point of alienating others, especially family members.

- But the Giver is much more than what he dispenses or has to give. We make a colossal mistake when we view the Giver only as a provider and miss the immense treasure Father has placed within the design of these wonderful people. Givers are created to release life and build community in the Church. In his great desire and ability to form community while always valuing individuals, a Giver's impartation of generational blessings is huge. I'm reminded of the commercial for a national credit card company that gives the price of many expensive items and vacations spots, then makes the statement, "Building the memories of a lifetime— Priceless." So it is with the Giver. When we look beyond the resources he can provide, we recognize the priceless value of the Giver.

Giver from a Mercy's Perspective

The Lord has such a sense of humor. One of the characteristics of a Giver is they do not want to be put in a box. Yet I have tried for days to put the Giver in a box in my outline. Somehow, it has not really pictured how I see the treasure of the Giver. So for this gift, I am basically abandoning much of my "box" and will simply write my perception of the Giver from a Mercy perspective.

When reading this portion, please do not assume all Givers have lots of money or great wealth. That is not the case. As we discuss resources, we are not talking about just finances but also resources of time, availability, "elbow grease," and his ability to see supplies that others miss.

In the past, I have judged the gift of Giver and have not seen the deep treasure hidden within this gift. When I asked the Lord to show me this treasure, here is what I heard:

The Lord: Don't expect from them. Give them grace at this point. Your expectation feels like bondage to them. Their need for freedom and independence is essential to Me. Because the other gifts can be manipulated emotionally to give financially, it is essential people cannot manipulate the one with whom I partner to steward My resources. Well-meaning human emotions interfere with My plans and interrupt what I am doing in My children's lives. Get the bigger picture. This is partnership with Me. As a Mercy gift, you partner with Me to pour on the healing oil. The Teacher partners with Me to bring truth in worship. The Prophet partners with Me to confront sin to free the sinner. The Giver partners with Me to provide or **not to provide** resources, the right gift at the right time. Is one gift more spiritual than another? Not in My eyes. All are in partnership with Me. All of this is My design.

You have not seen the giving of finances and provision as worship. Open your eyes to embrace worship in new paradigms. As each gift brings his anointing to the Altar of Sacrifice, it is high holy worship, and I receive it as a pleasing fragrance. To give a gift or not to give a gift is just has holy as a song, a prayer for deliverance, or a dance. It all smells the same at My altar.

Stop judging the heart of the Giver. When the Giver withholds, it may be by My plan. Yes, he has sin and blind spots like all of My children. Yes, he can manipulate his gift, just as you can as a Mercy. This is My call, not yours; it is My job to redeem him, not yours. I am merciful to Givers and forgive their sin. I delight in my Givers and so should you. See My image in them. I am the ultimate Giver. I gave.

Job got it right when he declared, 'You give and you take away.' When a Giver gives, you see it as from Me. But when he withholds resources, you criticize and do not see My image in this. This should not be! I give. I take away. It is all kindness from Me. Embrace it as from Me and see the Giver as My partner, not as your resource.

The mystery of the Giver reflects the mystery of God. Just when you think you know Me, I do something that mystifies you, and you realize you don't know Me at all. So it is with a Giver. You will never understand them. That too is My design. If you knew every move I was going to make, where would your faith be? I would be your size, not My size. I'm much bigger than you can imagine.

The Giver's mystery and flexibility keep others guessing. This attribute keeps others from always looking to the Giver for resources. Sometimes your expectation of a Giver is your way of trusting him rather than trusting Me. Newborns have all their needs met on their own timetable, but there is no maturity. Trusting Me, waiting on Me, looking to Me produces maturity. It is very important that My children look to Me for provision and not to a human Giver. Therefore, when I withhold through the Giver, it is Me speaking. It is the holy worship of the Giver to stand and say "No" when a "Yes" would be easier. I delight in the mystery of the Giver, and I won't let you define it or put it in a box.

Givers have a difficult dilemma. When they do not meet the expectations of others, people are disappointed. The Giver's ability to say "No" and walk away is My design. He can stand the tension. It is My protection. This is part of the mystery of the Giver and also part of the treasure.

Check out their homes. They are usually a mixture of old and new, reflecting their eclectic style. They connect the past to the present and the present to the future. They value the quality of well-made, functional pieces from the past and also enjoy the cutting-edge technology of the future. Old and new—generations connecting, even in their likes and dislikes.

I am the God of Abraham, Isaac, and Jacob, three generations. Givers reflect this part of My image. Leaving a legacy is important, and planning for the future is evidenced by their wills. Much of the time, they invest assets to be sure their resources keep on giving into the future. This is Me once again.

Always watching out for your future, always making note of what you like, always making sure you have what you need at the right time, I give wisely and well. I am the consummate Giver. Look at how I gave to David.

David had brought the Ark into Jerusalem. His heart's desire was to build Me a house. Seeing his heart, the superb Giver that I am said, "I hear your heart, David. You want to give something precious to Me. But you have already given Me your most precious possession, your whole heart. Now I will give you one of My best gifts. I know you are a Mercy gift, so I will design My gift specifically for you."

A Mercy gift desires:
1. To be the best, the first, the most intimate. God said, "I will make your name famous."
2. Alignment and a safe place. God said, "I will give you a safe homeland, secure borders, good judges. Your kingdom will be aligned correctly and well."
3. Not to be forgotten. God said, "I will give you a dynasty, an eternal dynasty."

Favor. God said, "I will never take My favor away from you."

Ruthie's perspective: This generosity totally overwhelmed David. God had read his heart and specifically gave him everything he had secretly longed for. God had watched him, had known him, and had strategically given to him, because David had given God everything He desired—his whole heart.

This is the call for the redeemed Giver: to partner with God and give a gift so well-planned and strategic that the recipient is delighted and overwhelmed, not so much with the actual gift, but overwhelmed at the thought and insight of the Giver. The Giver is appreciated, not just the gift. Yet again, this is God's image.

The Giver appreciates and relishes quality because of value. He sees value where others miss it. There is a song about an old violin being found and auctioned off. The auctioneer started with a one or two dollar bid. However, an old man, possibly a Giver, saw quality and value in this old violin. He stood and played a melody on it, revealing its value to others. The auctioneer changed his bid to one thousand dollars. This is the redeemed Giver's vision at its best, seeing quality and value not just in furniture but in people of all walks of life. Where others see the outward economic standing, the Giver looks deeper to see true worth. Recognizing this worth, he brings dignity and builds community by revealing this treasure to others. Making sure each individual is seen for his value is truly a God attribute.

After pulling the community together, the Giver enjoys stepping back to watch it work. It might be a mom Giver who cooks a sumptuous meal, invites all the family, and relishes the sight of them sitting around her table. She may not eat a bite. For her, standing at a distance and watching is fulfillment. God enjoys the same thing. Watching His kids play and work together brings Him such joy. That is the heart of a redeemed Giver.

Giver Characteristics as Seen in Bible Personalities

Job, Abraham, Cain, Matthew, Jacob, all Givers in the Bible, responded in different ways to the goodness and mercy of God.

Job

God was not angry with Job as many suppose. He loved Job but wanted him to have a much larger awareness of his Creator. If Job could get an idea of the vastness of God's power, His grandeur, and His provision, Job could be delivered from his fear, his need for control, and possibly his pride.

Job was a good man; widows rejoiced to see him coming; he did it right. But he lived a life of anxiety, concerned he might miss one jot or tittle, and then it would all be over for him. He was constantly trying to control, protect, and go behind to make sure everything was okay. Resources flowed to Job for God's purposes. Realizing this, Job stewarded this wealth well. But just in case God didn't come through, Job felt he should build yet another bigger barn.

God knew Job's character well and called him, "My servant Job." By allowing Satan to come against him, though not as punishment, God wanted to shift Job to a deeper place of faith, trust, and resources. One of the strongest statements a man can make in reference to his relationship to God is found in Job 13:15. In the middle of suffering and pain, Job, mighty man of God, makes a statement that echoes throughout the ages. "Though He slay me, yet will I trust Him!"

Embracing the pain, yet continuing to choose to trust God, Job becomes the standard for the Giver. Just as the Exhorter must know His character when there is no evidence He is present, so the Giver is called to trust God while embracing pain, stepping out in faith to wait until his needs are met, even if it is a long time coming.

At last, as Job was sitting in the ashes, destitute, with no resources left, God came. With great compassion and mercy, the Father spoke, "Job, look up. Look up here and see Me for who I am. See Me in all of My breathtaking wonder. Where were you when I flung the stars into space? Where were you when I stored up the snow and hail for battle? Job, look, see and be amazed at the glory and splendor of the heavens. See with new eyes all of creation, the deer giving birth, the giant whale leaping in the sea, the lion and bear with their young. Job, can you fathom how huge, how massive, how marvelous, how powerful I really am?"

God desired for Job to catch a glimpse of the magnitude of His abundance, to perceive that He, God, was the Supplier. He yearned for Job to be aware that all his prosperity came from God's hand, not from his own hard work.

Although Job was an excellent steward of his resources, fear and anxiety were robbing him of the pleasure and enjoyment of his blessings. He feared that he might not have enough, and he was anxious that he might lose it all.

God asked Job to compare his biggest barn to the vastness of the heavens, the seas, and all of creation. He wanted Job to realize his small bank account was nothing compared to the wealth of heaven.

As this revelation of the wealth and magnificence of God soaked into Job's weary heart and mind, so did the revelation of God's goodness, kindness, and love. Grasping the enormity of this staggering revelation, Job's heart was changed, and his faith shifted from fear to trust. Trust that God was indeed wealthy enough and powerful enough to supply all of his needs. Trust that God loved him and wanted to be his friend. No longer needing bigger barns and larger bank accounts, Job moved into recognizing his dependence upon the all-powerful, all-knowing, all-seeing Jehovah God. What comfort! What peace! What joy! What security! Job had heard of God, but now he saw Him.

As God restored above and beyond all he had in the beginning, Job could rest and enjoy his blessings. Realizing God was his friend, they could work together to meet the needs of Job's family and others. Job could now build community in a new way, based on God's riches and friendship rather than his own. God would furnish it, and Job would disperse it. It became a partnership, a relationship, and a friendship based on trust.

God wants His character reflected in the earth through us. Job did this. He made two statements that so reflect a redeemed, mature Giver.

"Though You slay me, yet will I trust You." Even if You never meet my needs, even though I am in more pain than I can imagine, I will trust You. I am totally in Your hands. I cannot and will not control my situation. You are in total control.

"You give and take away. Blessed be the name of the Lord." You are God and I am not. Your kindness is shown both in Your giving and in Your taking. Your character is good. The bigger picture is that when You give, I receive it as kindness because You know I need it. When You take away, I receive it as kindness because You know this is for my good. You never change, regardless of my needs or circumstances. Your kindness is shown in every situation. Taking away is just a different facet of Your kindness.

Abraham

Abraham was the father of nations, an instrument of life to the nation of Israel and eventually to the whole world. He believed God, stepped out in faith, and the rest is history. Abraham is a picture for Givers today.

The Giver releases life, but most of the time, he intends the life flow to be toward himself, to his benefit, his security, his advantage. To the carnal Giver, partial obedience is good enough. But to God, partial obedience is disobedience. However, we serve a long-suffering, merciful God, one Who is willing to wait and work on our behalf to bring us into full obedience so we can experience full blessing. So it was with Abram.

The Gift of Giver

Abram tended to control all situations and circumstances of his life for his own advantage. Sarah in Egypt, Hagar, and Ishmael exemplify his weakness. He was out for his best interest; he obeyed God, but on his own terms. God told him to leave his family and come out of Ur, and he did... sort of. As a Giver, he tended to obey but tweaked the circumstances just enough so it looked like obedience, but was really only half obedience. I repeat, to God half obedience is not really obedience.

Motivated by fear, Abram allowed Sarah to be known to Pharaoh as his sister. Technically she was Abram's half-sister, but, where Pharaoh was concerned, Abram was looking out for number one. However, as God's future friend began to discover the character of God and His faithfulness to His covenant and word, he received both a name change and a heart change. Abram became Abraham and began to live in the fullness of the Giver gift. Instead of working things out himself, he began to surrender to and trust Jehovah. Through his willingness to sacrifice his only son Isaac, Abraham obeyed God completely. Jehovah-Jireh rewarded this obedience by taking care of every detail and by providing a ram in the bush.

Abraham became God's friend. And such a friendship it was! He trusted the voice of the God of heaven, and they had lunch together. As they shared this covenant meal, they also shared their hearts. God told Abraham His plans concerning Sodom, and tenacious Giver Abraham asked God six times to spare the city. As they discussed this coming judgment, God heard His friend's heart and desire for Lot's safety. Shifting the circumstance of His judgment to exclude Abraham's family, God judged the city but spared Lot. Now that is relationship. It is knowing God face to face as a friend.

The temptation for the Giver is always to work it out for himself. Abraham knew God as a friend, believed His word that he would have a son. But he and Sarah simply worked it out for themselves. Givers want to live in peace with everyone, and Abraham was no exception.

Sarah had an idea. Abraham could sleep with Hagar, she would have a son, and they would adopt him. Problem solved. Non-confrontational Abraham must have thought it was a pretty good idea.

However, there came the day when this non-confrontational Giver had to make a stand. His birthright was to give life, build a legacy, and release generational blessings to a chosen nation. Eventually, these blessings would bring forth the One who would give life to all creation. In order to possess all God had promised, Abraham had to stop looking at his best option and step out in faith, taking a risk that God's way would work. He chose complete obedience. Abraham had to say "No" to his plans for Ishmael. He had to turn his back on Hagar. He had to rise up and fight five kings to save Lot. He had to take Isaac to Mount Moriah to meet God himself. Abraham had to sacrifice all of his dreams, his hopes, and his plans. There was no back-up plan, no alternative, no best option. Only total sacrifice of what he held most dear, his son.

Our Great Jehovah-Jireh met him there with a ram in the bush for His friend, Abraham. God now had Abraham's whole heart, and that was all he desired. Such a friend!

Selah! What a picture of our Great Giver God! He did the same for us! There was no back-up plan, no best option for our King. He met us at Mount Moriah and gave it all for us. He was the ram in the bush for us, because He wants to be our Friend, too.

Giver's Foundational Principle: Stewardship

The first mention of a tithe in scripture is connected with Abraham. He gave a tenth of all he had to Melchizedek, King of Salem, who foreshadowed Christ. Ten percent is the standard according to the mindset of the Giver. However, for both Job and Abraham, there came the day when God asked for it ALL. The question is, "Whose resources are they anyway?" Are they your resources to control, to measure out to others, to hoard because of fear? Or does it all belong to God, and you are his conduit pipe to release His resources to His body?

When the Giver realizes he must hold all things with an open hand, understanding it all belongs to God, he will move in the foundational principle of stewardship. He will realize God doesn't need his resources. He simply wants to be our Friend and our Partner. God is after our heart. He longs to partner with us to build His community and to release His life to the community around us. Friends discuss, friends share, and friends work together for the good of all. And that, Giver, is your call: To partner with the Creator of the Universe, building His community in the earth, using His resources in His timing and doing it in His way, with joy and celebration.

Giver's Birthright:
To Be Generationally Life-giving

"A grateful heart prepares the way for the Giver." To be generationally life-giving and to invoke life-giving generational blessing for family and for the community is the birthright of the Giver.

The humility and gratitude that come when the Giver understands the immensity of God, His goodness, and His ability to supply his need prepare the way for God's mercy and goodness to be released into the earth realm. In Matthew Jesus prayed, "Let your kingdom come on earth as it is in heaven." Only after the Giver intimately knows and understands the wealth and character of God from heaven's perspective is he released into a realm of supernatural stewardship. From this position, Kingdom resources become generationally life-giving to build Kingdom communities in the earth.

The Giver is called to connect, network, and build life-giving Kingdom community, creating a place of nurture for new life and multiplication. This new life can take many forms. It can be spiritual birth through salvation, the coming alongside new ministries in intercession, or hovering over new businesses with the needed resources to see them thrive and come to maturity. The Giver's biggest impact is found at this point. He recognizes that although his nurture has helped bring maturity, he must now release control and allow God to shift the emerging ministry, business, or disciple from the care and nurture of the Giver into the maturity of God's purposes.

Fifth Day of Creation

Genesis 1:20-23. "Then God said, 'Let the waters abound with an abundance of living creatures, and let birds fly above the earth across the face of the firmament of the heavens.' So God created great sea creatures and every living thing that moves, with which the waters abounded, according to their kind, and every winged bird according to its kind. And God saw that it was good. And God blessed them, saying, 'Be fruitful and multiply, and fill the waters in the seas, and let birds multiply on the earth.' So the evening and the morning were the fifth day."

Diversity and Celebration! Birth, nurture, protection, community, and interaction all came into earth on the fifth day. We see life in a new form. On the third day, there were trees. The seed formed in the fruit of the slow-growing tree, fell to the ground, then emerged as a new tree, totally separate from the old. No further interaction occurred, nor was it necessary.

Not so on the fifth day. On this day, we see life in extraordinarily new manifestations of God's creativity. Physical live birth came into the earth. Life and death emerged in a new dimension. New sounds, new colors, and new movement were seen. A huge leap forward in creation came as life flowed through the blood. And generations were released through multiplication.

The diversity was incredible. A hummingbird looks nothing like a penguin or an ostrich. And a salmon does not resemble in the least an oyster or an eel. Whales, sharks, conchs, clown fish, and stingrays are all fish. Blue birds, cardinals, emu, storks, and even albatross are all birds. All are so different, yet easily identified. They are all fifth-day creatures. Flocks of birds, gaggles of geese, and schools of fish, all flowing in community and communicating constantly, move about, swim, fly, hop, and even dance. What an amazing, creative God we serve! His fingerprints exploded in creativity on the fifth day. Can you feel His joy as He shouted in celebration, "Go and multiply! Fill the earth and seas with songs, shouts, and movement. Even dance!"

It was at this point that God released the first blessing. As He examined His work on the other days of creation, He had proclaimed, "Now, that is good!" But today was exceptionally grand. Today He blessed the work of His hands. Blessings are a unique download of a tiny spark of God's goodness toward the one being blessed, impacting people, communities, and generations. And on the fifth day God released His first blessing.

This first blessing is the blessing of multiplication. Multiplication of life. The Giver's first call is to release, multiply, and bless life, joining with and participating in the joy of the Creator's celebration of community and life.

Don't you love to watch birds building nests, singing as they flit from branch to branch? It is thrilling to watch as the new fledglings fly from the nest, suddenly becoming independent and needing no further interaction with their family. Or so I thought.

Recently, I have discovered a whole new dynamic about birds and even fish. Yes, they build nests. Yes, they nurture and sacrifice for their young. But there is a much higher call for the birds of the fifth day. They sing, and they communicate. They interact with all of creation. And creation interacts with them. They build community.

Recent articles published in Animal Communication Networks (Cambridge University Press) at Cornell University, noted that scientists are now beginning to understand bird songs on a much deeper level.[2] Birds, by their singing, create community. Once we thought that each species of birds had a few, distinct songs, all the same, all repetitive. But now we know there is so much more to bird melodies. Researchers have found that one particular banded wren was documented to have over 96 different songs. Each song communicated a specific message. His song could identify individual families, and some songs were intended for his family only. Other songs communicated information to the general bird community, such as the location of the best food sources, or marked the boundaries of territories. The best songs, however, seem to have no particular purpose except to express pure joy.

The most intriguing song is the dawn chorus, released to literally awaken the morning. As dew falls on the leaves of the trees or blades of grass at night, it rests there, waiting for daybreak. When the first song breaks through the stillness of the shadows of early morning, the cells of the leaves begin to open in response to the sound vibrations. This opening causes the dew to be absorbed into the leaf, thus nurturing and releasing life to the whole plant. This interaction of creation is phenomenal.

Selah! Oh, Lord, our God, how majestic is Your name in all the earth! Your creation shouts Your glory, Your splendor, Your greatness, Your wisdom. Give us eyes to see and ears to hear!

For years, we've been aware of the whale songs, although their long distance communication skills are still such a mystery to us. But now oceanographers are beginning to study the sounds, grunts, clicks, and growls of the haddock and other fish of the sea. Who knew that even fish release sound and build community through communication? Have you ever watched a school of fish moving in the water? Talk about synchronized swimming! That is intricate communication and community.

But what has this to do with the Giver gift? Everything. The Exhorter communicates and moves masses of people, but the Giver uses communication to network, to draw people together to form individual communities or tribes, or flocks or schools, or gaggles. The list goes on. Just as the birds and fish were created to sing and build community, so the Giver is called to release life and joy all around him in myriads of ways. His networking skills are unsurpassed, and his ability to attract diverse groups of people and pull them together as community is exceptional.

Nurturing, sacrificing, and protecting their young when necessary, birds and Givers are an expression of the nature of God. Just as birds and even a few fish hover over the nest, feed their young, and then release them into their destiny, so, too, is the call of the Giver. His portion is to hover over the new birth in intercession or with resources, whether it is a new business or ministry, incubate it until the right moment, then release it, pushing it out of the nest to fly on its own.

Birds' nesting and mating habits display such variety, as does the Giver in his array of projects, venues, and interests. The fifth day is a beautiful reflection of the Giver and his extraordinary ability to network, communicate, and celebrate life by connecting us all in wonderful ways.

One of the new buzzwords in the Church is life groups. And that, my friend, is exactly what the Giver does so well. Whether a five-minute conversation at the checkout of the grocery store, or a Tuesday night gathering of the Church, the Giver can create a life group extraordinaire, giving life to those around him. I love that about Givers. Celebrating life wherever they go, they invite us all to splash around in the joy with them.

Jehovah-Rohe

("Raah" is the word for shepherd. However, I found that in most of the lists of the compound names of Jehovah, the name "Rohe" is used which denotes the pastoral aspect of the word for shepherd or Raah.)

Psalm 23. "The Lord is my shepherd; I shall not want. He makes me to lie down in green pastures; He leads me beside the still waters. He restores my soul; He leads me in the paths of righteousness for His name's sake. Yea, though I walk through the valley of the shadow of death, I will fear no evil; For You are with me; Your rod and Your staff, they comfort me. You prepare a table before me in the presence of my enemies; You anoint my head with oil; My cup runs over. Surely goodness and mercy shall follow me all the days of my life; And I will dwell in the house of the Lord forever."

More than any other gift, the Giver needs much reassurance of his safety and security; therefore, the compound name of Jehovah for this gift is Jehovah-Rohe, our Good Shepherd of Psalm 23.

The Lord is my shepherd, I shall not want. Knowing God for His faithfulness builds a security for the Giver to give him confidence that this Good Shepherd will supply all his needs according to His riches in glory.

He makes me to lie down in green pastures. Only when he is fully convinced in his spirit that God is in control, and He is big enough to take care of all his needs, will the Giver lie down and rest from his multitude of projects and people.

He leads me beside still waters. Sheep are not very good swimmers. Their wool is thick and will quickly absorb water. This hazard can set up a recipe for drowning. Swiftly moving water would be a dangerous place for sheep to drink. But the Good Shepherd knows this. After all, He created the sheep and knows his fear. So He leads him beside still water for a drink. When the only water available is running water, the Shepherd scoops up the water and gives him a drink from His own hand.

The Good Shepherd knows the dangers and fears the Giver faces. He goes ahead of him to make a place of quiet waters so he can drink deeply of the Living Water of life, even from His own hand. Oh, how He loves the Giver! Oh, how He understands him, his fear and anxiety, his need for control. But oh, how He longs to be his friend! To eat a covenant meal with him like he did with Abraham, to share His heart with him, to have the Giver know Him intimately, face to face.

When his life is out of control, and he cannot provide all he needs, the Giver must quickly run to his Shepherd. Run to Him, spend time with Him, get to know Him face to face. God wants to be the Giver's BFF (Best Friend Forever). Then this precious Giver can partner with the Creator of the Universe to change nations, birth new ministries, and see His Kingdom advanced in the world around him. In this place of peace and rest his soul will be restored.

There will be no compromise in his life style, because he understands God is the Supplier, not himself. Never breaching any lines of integrity with halfway obedience, the Giver can live in full confidence, trusting the Lord that he will be in the right place at the right time with the right provision, because he is with the right Shepherd.

He can walk through the valley of the shadow of death, because his friend, the Good Shepherd, is with him.

Your rod and staff are a comfort. While visiting with a local shepherd several years ago, he showed me his rod. It was an ominous looking club. He told me sheep are literally hardheaded, and sometimes he had to "bop" them on the head to let them know he is trying to lead them, but they are not following. For some of his sheep, however, he only has to lay this club on their neck, and they respond quickly to the touch of his rod to follow their shepherd.

When he did have to "bop" them, it was not because he was upset or wanted to punish them. It was to make sure they stayed on the path he had chosen for them or to keep them from eating or drinking substances that were not good for them. His rod was a comfort because it was a sign that he was near and was watching out for their good.

When the sheep dog got a little "nippy," the shepherd could use the rod to protect his sheep. What a Good Shepherd we have. The Giver can also be a little hard-headed at times. He can be relentless, never giving up easily. If this hard-headedness is focused against the will of the Shepherd, He will discipline him so the Giver remembers who is really in charge.

He prepares a table, a communion table. It cost our Good Shepherd a high price to set this table, but He says to the Giver and to all of us, "You are worth it!" As a Giver looks at the cost of this table and the immensity of the Shepherd's love for him, he has a choice:

- He can turn away with the attitude of "I deserve all I get and I can supply all of my needs. I choose not to become vulnerable."
- Or in all humility, he can bow low at the cross, become vulnerable, and with a grateful heart kneel at this table. As the enemies of the Shepherd watch this extravagant display of His boundless love and commitment to this one, they realize once again their powerlessness to harm His sheep.

Then out of His mercy and grace, the Shepherd pours His oil, His anointing, on the Giver and releases so much living water, so much life, that it spills over on all around him. From this place of overflow the Giver releases the blessings of God's grace everywhere he goes. Life springs up all around him. A trail of mercy and goodness is left for others to follow and discover where our Lover keeps his sheep (Song of Solomon). That is evangelism at its finest for the Giver.

I have asked several Givers what their greatest fear might be, and I have been surprised at their answers. Three of the five interviewed answered the same way, "That I would die needy and poor." The Great Shepherd knew this, too, because in this psalm He spoke of having no fear of death, that goodness and mercy would follow the Giver all of his days, and that he would dwell in God's house forever. Such comfort, such peace. Such a Shepherd.

When the Giver finds his security, provision, and safety in Jehovah-Rohe, our Good Shepherd, and responds in holiness from his heart, the payoff is generationally extravagant.

The Altar of Incense

The Altar of Incense bathed the whole Tabernacle with the pleasant scent of perfectly mixed spices. It released a smoky haze, similar to the cloud that hovered above the Tabernacle by day. This haze and fragrance covered and connected everything in the Tabernacle with worship. The fire to burn at this table came from the Brazen Altar at the entrance. The cleansing of sin, the complete sacrifice, and fullness of forgiveness was echoed throughout as the burning of the incense filled the atmosphere with the sweet-smelling aroma of worship and intercession. This double anointing is key for the Giver.

Romans 12:1 says everything we do, our lifestyle, is our reasonable worship. The Giver's worship is carried out in a multitude of ways, small and large. His networking skills, honed to perfection, are part of his worship. Giving generously, freely, and with a happy heart is also worship for him. Like the fragrance of incense in the Tabernacle, the Giver's worship permeates the Church, not only covering them with intercession in the spiritual realm but also many times in the physical realm through needs being met by using the Lord's resources.

Intercession flows from a heart of gratitude. As the priest lit the incense, he was commanded to remember the works of the Lord. As the Giver lives a lifestyle of worship, celebrating God's fingerprints daily, and being grateful for all His provision, he empowers his authority in intercession.

Giver Stronghold and Root Iniquity: Ownership

God's design and the Giver's birthright is his understanding that God is the owner of all of his resources. God is the Provider, and the only thing the Giver needs to do is pray to discover to whom or where the resources need to go. Very simple, no problem here. The Giver can release the resources, giving life, creating community, and moving on.

The contention comes when there is no clear view of who provides and who owns the resources. Because God has designed the Giver to see resources others miss and to have instinctive timing related to finances, the Giver can come under the delusion that perhaps the accrued resources are at his own disposal. Indeed, he should be the one to make the heady decisions to release or not release the resources when a particular need arises in the Church.

Actually, this contention goes much deeper than finances or resources. The bottom line is the Giver believes he has the right to choose his own destiny and do whatever he wants with his life. Believing he can supply all his own needs, he feels no need for God, and possibly God should be obliged to him for his supply. This wrong belief is the stronghold of the giver.

The contention over ownership produces three iniquitous patterns. The first mindset produces an arrogance that declares, "I can use my resources in any manner I see fit. After all, I was wise with my decisions; I worked hard for what I have. This stuff is mine, and I will choose to spend or not to spend my reserve according to my pleasure."

Cain was possibly a Giver. He wanted to offer to God what he wanted to offer. He knew from his parents that God required a blood sacrifice. But after all, he was an excellent farmer. He tilled the earth, watered it, and harvested it. It was his to give or withhold. In his pride he gave, very religiously, what he chose to give. Obedience is better than sacrifice. Cain did not believe that God valued his sacrifice. But God was not looking for religious activity or even sacrifice. He was looking for relationship, a relationship that could come only through humility and blood sacrifice.

When the Giver or his gift is not valued, he moves toward an independent spirit or pride by turning away and leaving. Projects are aborted; destinies are lost. Cain was looking for his best option, what would work best for him. Thinking his way was the best, he could not see the bigger picture of relationship. Yes, the Giver's design is flexibility, and a better option may come along. But there are times when the Lord calls the Giver simply to obey.

A second mindset found in the Giver gives birth to a spirit of control. "I can use my assets," he says, "to control my children, my church, my team, my life, and the lives of others around me." From this place the Giver will begin to give strategic gifts to strategic individuals to assert control over decisions or directions he feels should be made. Wonderful gifts, but there are strings attached. Very rarely will any words be spoken as to direction or decision, but the spirit of control is evident as the gift is given. Although the Giver prefers not being identified as a "Giver" in a group, it seems that those in community with them are aware of their availability of resources and will watch facial expressions, will listen to their words, and will try to vote or agree with the opinion of the Giver. Jesus said in Matthew 10:6, "Freely you have received, freely give." Again it is a question of ownership. Is it God's or the Giver's?

The third Giver mindset is the saddest of all. It presents itself as fear—fear of not having enough, fear that God might not come through to provide, and especially fear in the presence of pain.

When is enough, enough? Realizing his own inability to provide for himself and those who depend upon him, the Giver works increasingly hard to store up in order to make sure he has enough, in case he might need it. The "what if" question looms strongly in his mind as he continues to seek after more, unable to trust the One who says, "And my God shall supply all your need according to His riches in glory by Christ Jesus." Philippians 4:19.

Job was in this position until he realized how big and glorious God's riches really are. Abraham got a glimpse of this truth as the kings of the earth continued to show him favor and bring him gifts. Although David was not a Giver, I believe the Lord had the Giver in mind as he penned Psalm 23. In answer to the Giver's question of "what if?" all of heaven resounds with "Nevertheless, GOD!!!"

What if I have a need I cannot meet? Nevertheless, the Good Shepherd will supply all of your needs according to His riches in glory.

But what if I face death? Nevertheless, your Good Shepherd will be with you, comfort you, and feed you, even in the presence of your enemies.

What if I grow old and cannot supply for myself? Nevertheless, His goodness and mercy will follow you, catch up to you, and overtake you so that you will dwell in His house forever.

So many "what if's" abound, but there is always a "Nevertheless, God!" for the Giver to rely on.

Time with Father

Givers can give resources willingly, freely, and see some good fruit from this giving. But Givers were created for much, much more. Created to give life, he cannot give what he does not possess. Without an intimate relationship with Father, he has no real life to give.

The birth process is painful, but the end result is life. For a Giver, this is the required process he must go through to release life.

As he spends time with the Good Shepherd of Psalm 23, although the Shepherd may direct the path of the Giver thru difficult places, it will be places of learning to trust, even in the face of pain. God calls him to be put at risk as he dines in the presence of his enemies. These enemies are bound and chained by the power of the blood of Jesus, but they are still present. Only by continually gazing into the face of his Friend, Jesus, and listening to His voice will the enemy's taunts be drowned out. Then the Giver's eyes will be filled with the goodness and love of the Shepherd.

Called to celebrate despite pain as he walks through the valley of the shadow of death, a Giver can enjoy the security and joy of his Father. It could be physical death, but there are other deaths that are quite painful. The death to selfish desires, the death of a relationship held dear, or the death of dreams and hopes can be just as painful.

God does not promise there will be no death, but He does promise the Giver He will be there with him, comforting him with His rod and His staff, guarding and guiding him all the way. The Father understands his need of security and promises never to leave or forsake him.

Abraham knew God face to face. Job saw Him in all His glorious splendor. This Good Shepherd so longs for you to know him, too. Not just as provider, although He is that. His heart for you, Giver, is to know him as friend. His BFF! (Best Friend Forever)

But what happens to you, Giver, when you cannot meet your own needs, or anyone else's for that matter. What happens when the only resource left to you is to become vulnerable, admit your need, and even beg your enemy for help? And what happens when there is no trustworthy source of security to be found?

Take heart, Giver, for on that Passover day Jesus thought of you. He could see you as you stood in the place of need, a place where you could not grasp the faith to trust your Father one more time, the place of Job's pain, sitting in ashes and waiting. He knew there would be that day for you, Giver. So the One who knew no need chose to become impoverished and destitute, just for you.

Jesus as Giver

During Jesus' ministry on earth, He gave wisely and well. Understanding stewardship, He knew it all belonged to His Father and trusted Him for all His needs to be met. Jesus declared, "Foxes have holes, and birds have nests, but the Son of Man has no place to lay His head."

He prayed for His daily bread and trusted His Father to supply His provisions, including a place of rest, food, and even his tax bill. Remember the coin in the fish's mouth? Miraculously feeding the multitudes, He formed community through supernatural provision.

Jesus appreciated the value of each individual and built a tightly knit community made up of a tax collector, uneducated fishermen, and even a Pharisee or two. Seeing past their social status, He gave them dignity by recognizing their place of worth in His band of disciples.

As a Giver, He understood Kingdom finances. He explained the widow's mite and the faith that accompanied this act from a Kingdom perspective.

Jesus committed. He did not opt out when circumstances grew difficult. Making the decision before the foundation of the world, the cross was not a last minute choice. Keeping His commitment, even when it was not His easiest option, Jesus waited in pain because He saw the value in His creation and in His kids. He saw the value in you. So He gave.

"For God so loved the world that He gave His only begotten Son, that whoever believes in Him should not perish but have everlasting life." John 3:16. This Great Giver connected all the dots. Through His life, death, and resurrection, He connected the past to the present, and the present to the future, leaving a legacy which continues today.

Selah! When I reflect on what He gave, how He gave it so freely, and how great was His sacrifice, I can hardly contain my gratitude! It brings me low, and I am undone in His mercy. Thank You, Jesus, that You gave.

The Last Words of Jesus on the Cross: "I thirst."

Givers have a passion to give life. They develop the principle of stewardship by using someone else's (God's) resources to build someone else's (God's) work. Being "needy" is the most devastating state imaginable for them.

Jesus, our Great Giver, had the best to give and all of the resources of creation were at His disposal. Driven by a passion to give life, He chose to become vulnerable, even down to the most basic of all human need, thirst.

At this point on the day of the cross, Jesus was exhausted, beaten, and greatly dehydrated. He needed water.

He knew much about water. He had hovered over it on the first day, separated it on the second day, and divided it on the third day. He had commanded it, parted it, fished in it, was baptized in it, and even walked on it. With one simple word, He could have called the water of heaven to come flooding down, pouring over His thirsty body in abundant rain. But He chose to wait in pain for His Father's hand to move.

Recognizing that all good gifts come from His Father, regardless of who He uses to furnish them, He begged water from the hand of the very enemy who was crucifying Him.

I thirst.

And this enemy could choose to give him a drink, or not.

And He continued to trust His Father to meet His need, or not!

He became thirsty so that He could give you, Giver, the water of life!

He became destitute so that you could know, "My God shall supply all of my needs according to His riches in glory," even if He uses the hand of your enemy to supply it.

The Treasure of the Giver

Giver, forever a mystery, you carry the incense, the very fragrance of God's heart. Your destiny is to give this fragrance to the world. Just as myrrh must be crushed and incense must be burned to release their essence, so you must become vulnerable and needy before Him to allow Him to release His good gifts through you.

A joy to be around, you draw others into your celebration and build wonderful community by communicating to them your Source of supply, His storehouse. Seeing and valuing the uniqueness of those around you, you cause us to experience that fragrance of Him who has so captured your heart. Trusting Him to supply all your needs, even to the final minute, to the last penny, to the one remaining drop of water, you reveal to the world this Great Shepherd from Whom all blessings flow.

As you lavish generational blessings into your family line and splash life on all around, you build Kingdom community at every opportunity. You are known, not for your resources, but as a friend of God.

Chapter Seven
The Gift of Ruler

Motto of the Ruler: Git 'er done!

"We can take a deep breath and relax, dad is here, and he always has the plan." This is the security that the Ruler gift, male or female, brings. He sees the "How?" The redeemed Ruler carries an innate sense of authority and responsibility that brings peace into situations because he always has a plan and a way to accomplish what is needed for the group, whether it is a building, organization, or a social network. It is in his DNA to plan it, build it, and implement it. Just as Nehemiah took broken, ordinary people and attained supernatural results when he rebuilt the wall around Jerusalem, the Ruler can build God's Kingdom or establish a social structure as he synergistically releases life to those under his authority.

Ruler Characteristics

- Relationship and loyalty drive the Ruler. When backing a visionary, he will push hard to complete the project. I've heard leaders say, "I love Rulers. I know they always have my back!" However, if he believes the leader does not need him or is disloyal to him, many times he will decide to quit and look for another person to carry on the project.

- On the other side, he honors loyalty from those under him more than their competence. Carrying the highest anointing for fathering, he calls forth the best in people and causes the ordinary and broken to rise to a level of extraordinary accomplishment. Looking again at Nehemiah as he rebuilt the wall of Jerusalem. He finished in record time and established a social structure by releasing hope and vision to the returning Jewish exiles.

- Catching a vision for God's Kingdom, the Ruler significantly expands it. Although not necessarily a nurturer or one who is into details, the ruler's DNA is to plan it, build it, and implement it. A predatory mindset of loving projects while using people can empower a predator/victim stronghold in the unrighteous Ruler, and cause wounding to those under his leadership. However, as the Ruler pays the price to stop and consult with the Father about how to nurture while he builds, he shifts into using the project as a way of loving and nurturing people. In so doing, he releases spiritual and generational blessings and exemplifies the Father Heart of God.

- How do you eat an elephant? One bite at the time. By breaking jobs down into doable tasks, the Ruler gets things done in a timely manner. Owning his own problems and never playing the blame game, he declares, "Don't cry over spilled milk," and simply fixes it, and moves on to the next project.

- Working under pressure motivates him. Skilled in inspiring others, he seems to believe that they do a better job under pressure also. This pressure can cause an ethics breach just to "get it done" and may leave the details unfinished because of unmet deadlines. An 80% completion of a job may seem good enough in contrast to the Prophet, who makes sure every "i" is dotted and every "t" is crossed. The Ruler has high administrative skills and, when coupled with a Giver, can have a massive impact.

The Gift of Ruler

Ruler Characteristics as Seen in Bible Personalities

Nehemiah, wall builder; Solomon, king of Israel; Joseph, Pharaoh's assistant; Noah, master ship builder; Boaz, kinsman-redeemer all exhibited characteristics of the Ruler grace gift.

Solomon

Solomon, son of Bathsheba, grew up in David's household. His brother Absalom tried to usurp their father's kingdom. His brother Adonijah proclaimed himself king when their father was on his deathbed. However, God chose Solomon to succeed David as king.

Before Solomon's birth, David was completely broken over his sin with Bathsheba. Perhaps that is why David was careful to mentor Solomon in the ways of the Lord. King David, with his gift of Mercy, had a heart for worship and an immense desire to see that worship permeate his whole kingdom. He brought worship to its highest level in the tabernacle, ushering in the sound of music and singing to honor and extol the greatness of Jehovah, God of the Universe. But because he was a man of war, he was not allowed to build the temple. As a Ruler gift, Solomon carried an innate ability to see how to get the job done. Because he was a loyal son and a man of peace, he was chosen for the job.

I believe as David instructed Solomon in how the temple should be built, he also imparted to his son an awe of God and instilled in him an understanding of true worship. Solomon would know the "how" and the "why." This insight would give him the vision and the understanding of how to display the magnificence of God for the entire world to see.

Chosen for such an overwhelming task, he understood that he could not get the job done alone, so he asked for help. He asked for wisdom, and God gave it so abundantly that Solomon was known as the wisest man in the earth.

And Solomon built the temple.

Wisdom and worship. What a combination! Stop for a moment and imagine with me the glorious sound of perfect harmony as the trained musicians and singers declared the majesty of Jehovah during the dedication of Solomon's temple. Add to that the pungent aromas of incense, freshly baked bread, and burning flesh from the sacrifices at the altar. Totally immersed in the peace and beauty of Jehovah Shalom as He descended on them, the people experienced His presence so weighty even the priests could not stand.

It is no wonder the world was drawn to Jerusalem. God put eternity in the hearts of men, according to Ecclesiastes 3:11, and Eternity began to call men to Jerusalem to honor His name.

And they came.

But true to his DNA, Solomon continued to build. He became so caught up in the urgency of his continuous building projects that he neglected his most important privilege of spending time in this glorious temple, gazing upon the beauty of the Lord as his father David had done.

The world continued to come to Jerusalem. But what did they come to see? The city Solomon built was wonderful, as were his stables, horses, and gardens. What did he show the kings and queens who came? As they marveled at Solomon's wisdom, did he reveal the true source of his wisdom, the Ancient of Days?

Solomon had built well. He had networked people to build a social and economic structure and leave a legacy of reform and buildings that comprised his earthly kingdom. What he did was good, but the good is always the enemy of the best. His wives and concubines had drawn him away from his first love by enticing him to build pagan temples. In the end, he was frustrated and disillusioned because he never completed the 'one thing' he was called to do.

With worship in the temple at its highest level, he had the capacity to release the glory of God to the entire known world. He missed an opportunity for the world to see a kingdom of priests living, moving, and worshiping the one true God. The 'one thing' he was called to do was release spiritual, generational blessing in the earth. In the life of Solomon, this call was left unfulfilled. The wisest man in all the earth failed in integrity and fell into immorality and idolatry. Solomon missed it by 20%.

Yes, Rulers are called to build. However, the project, whether a wall or a kingdom, is only a platform from which to do the 'one thing' they were created to do—reveal the Father Heart of God and release spiritual blessings to the generations.

Positioned to release this blessing, Solomon did not deal with issues in his sons. He left generational curses that were never broken off the lineage of the kings of Israel. After his death, part of the Kingdom was torn from his bloodline, never to be restored until Yeshua Jesus comes to bring full restoration to the nation of Israel.

Nehemiah

Because of his loyalty to leadership, his "always got your back" mentality, and his faithfulness to get the job done, Nehemiah was chosen by King Artaxerxes, the king of Persia, to be his Cupbearer. In this position, Nehemiah stood by the king daily to offer him a cup of wine. It was one of the most trusted offices in the kingdom. When the king noticed Nehemiah's sad countenance, Nehemiah was straightforward about the cause with no hint of manipulation or welfare mentality. He knew his task, understood what he needed for it, and was not afraid to ask. Because of his great favor with the king, Nehemiah received permission to go to Jerusalem and was granted provision for the trip.

Arriving in Jerusalem, he surveyed the city and saw the broken walls and burned gates. Undaunted in the face of such a huge undertaking, Nehemiah formed a plan. There was much opposition to his plan, but Nehemiah's face was set like flint. Amid rumors, ridicule, and resistance, he continued to build the wall and restore the gates of the city. His strategy to build with a tool in one hand and a weapon in the other encouraged the people. He was on the scene, worked with the people, and did what was necessary to get the job done. His confidence in God and his physical presence brought comfort and security to those around him.

The sound of the shofar brought immediate help to their portion of the wall, thus creating a safe environment for the people to work without concern. This safety zone is a wonderful picture of a redeemed Ruler. Nehemiah took wounded, broken people, networked and nurtured them to accomplish a supernatural task, and rebuilt the wall of Jerusalem in record time.

Nehemiah was known primarily as the rebuilder of the wall, but he did not stop there. As a governmental official, he worked with Ezra, the priest, to bring justice to the poor and social reform to the nation. He also put into place an ongoing plan for the provision of the temple and priests.

Even at the end of his life, Nehemiah returned to Jerusalem to make sure the people were still following these reforms. When he found that they were not, he again took the necessary steps to insure provision for the coming generations. That, Ruler, is a generational father's heart toward a nation.

Selah! Thank You, Father, for men like Nehemiah, who are still fathering the generations.

Ruler's Foundational Principle: Holiness, Integrity, and Nurture

To manifest the heart of the Father is the call and destiny of the Ruler gift. The question the Ruler must ask himself is, "Whose kingdom am I building?"

The Gift of Ruler

In answering this question, the principles are clearly defined. A lifestyle of righteousness, nurture, and embracing the holiness of God are the requirements for building God's Kingdom:
- Integrity at the highest level, never cutting corners, or skipping details.
- Giving back more than he takes.

The clarion call for the Ruler is loving people and using the project as a means to launch others into their destiny.

Ruler's Birthright: To be a Spiritual Life-giver

"Historically, this gift has been the most compromised, but God is concerned with redeeming the concept of Fatherhood which the devil has warped."[3] God wants to restore the Ruler to what He intended. Jesus said, "When you have seen Me, you have seen the Father." John 14:9.

As the Ruler submits to God, leaning on Him rather than on his own natural leadership ability, and lives in holiness, integrity and nurture, he will be a shining example of what the Father Heart of God looks like in everyday life.

Sixth Day of Creation

Genesis 1:24-31. "Then God said, 'Let the earth bring forth the living creature according to its kind: cattle and creeping thing and beast of the earth, each according to its kind'; and it was so. [25] And God made the beast of the earth according to its kind, cattle according to its kind, and everything that creeps on the earth according to its kind. And God saw that it was good.

[26] "Then God said, 'Let Us make man in Our image, according to Our likeness; let them have dominion over the fish of the sea, over the

birds of the air, and over the cattle, over all the earth and over every creeping thing that creeps on the earth.' ²⁷So God created man in His own image; in the image of God He created him; male and female He created them. ²⁸Then God blessed them, and God said to them, 'Be fruitful and multiply; fill the earth and subdue it; have dominion over the fish of the sea, over the birds of the air, and over every living thing that moves on the earth.'

²⁹ "And God said, 'See, I have given you every herb that yields seed which is on the face of all the earth, and every tree whose fruit yields seed; to you it shall be for food. ³⁰Also, to every beast of the earth, to every bird of the air, and to everything that creeps on the earth, in which there is life, I have given every green herb for food'; and it was so. ³¹ Then God saw everything that He had made, and indeed it was very good. So the evening and the morning were the sixth day."

This day was the "TADA!" of the creation week, bringing all the other five days into perspective.

Great diversity marked the sixth day of creation. Many types of animals, insects, and reptiles were created.

On this day God created man.

A new kind of life was established in the earth: spiritual life.

God literally breathed His own Spirit into the man He had labored over, formed, and shaped. In the Genesis account describing the sixth day, we see on the first five days God spoke, and it came to be. However, as He made the creatures and man on the sixth day, we find different Hebrew words to describe His activity. Rather than calling forth light and life, He literally "made" these creatures.

As God created the animals, the Hebrew word indicates He made or commanded the earth to bring them forth. But a much more specific word is used when He created Adam. It is a word meaning to squeeze and mold into a shape, much like a potter creates with his hands.

Jehovah Elohim, the Self-existent God, the Supreme Magistrate or Judge of the Universe, used His hands. He stretched, squeezed, and shaped us into His image. Breathing His very own Spirit into us, we became a living man, spirit, soul, and body. On this day, we looked like God Himself, filled with His light, His glory, and His Ruach breath or Spirit.

The five days before this day were simply the backdrop for the crown of His creation, man himself. The earth in all of its beauty and splendor was fashioned as a dwelling place perfectly suited for Adam. This terrestrial ball was to be the meeting place for God to have relationship with His friends Adam and Eve. Together they would form community with God, become His bride, and share intimacy with the Father, Son, and Holy Spirit.

And God said, "This is very good."

In my own words, it could have gone something like this: "Wow! This is my most joyful day. This is my best idea!" God laughed and shouted.

"At last, I have a wonderful, delightful friend, a son, with whom I can stroll and converse, sit and share, laugh, sing, dance, and celebrate."

Then, turning to Adam, He smiled as only a proud Papa can and presented the Garden to His son. "Adam, look around you. See all that I have made just for you to enjoy. It is all yours. Eat any of the juicy, delicious fruit you find and check out the vegetables, crunchy and savory. The grains? I love fresh bread, so I'll show you how to grind it and bake it. We can share a loaf while we talk in the afternoons.

"All those creatures moving around or swimming in the sea are at your command. So let's take a stroll and look, laugh, and delight in all that I have given you. It's all so good.

"And Adam every afternoon in the quiet of the day, I'll come, and we can have a heart-to-heart chat, just you and Me. You can tell Me how you chuckled at the mating rituals of the birds, how your beans are putting on new sprouts, or we can just sit and enjoy each other's presence. Any questions? I'll have answers for you. This is gonna be great, Adam. This is gonna be very good."

As they built relationship, Adam basically just enjoyed being with his Father. During their time together God was imparting spiritual fatherhood to him so that in generations to come, men and women would have an imprint of Jehovah Elohim and of Abba Father.

From this place of communion came the authority to release spiritual blessings. It was that communion, that relationship, that community which Adam was to go and multiply.

Father God has not changed in His call or diminished our authority over creation. Yet, we have not understood our mandate given in the Garden. It is still there. This mandate so reflects the Ruler's call to administer, lead, and nurture people and to build God's Kingdom in His way with his father anointing. In the Garden, God did not do it for Adam, but He gave him the tools with which to do it. So it is with the Ruler. You have the tools and the anointing. Go, build relationship, and spiritually father the generations.

Jehovah-Tsidkenu

Jeremiah 23:4-6 (The Message) "I'll set shepherd-leaders over them who will take good care of them. They won't live in fear or panic anymore. All the lost sheep rounded up!" God's Decree. "Time's coming"—God's Decree—"when I'll establish a truly righteous David-Branch, A ruler who knows how to rule justly. He'll make sure of justice and keep people united. In his time Judah will be secure again and Israel will live in safety. This is the name they'll give him: 'God-Who-Puts-Everything-Right.'"

As a child, I remember hearing my mom say, "Just wait until your daddy comes home!" Sometimes it was because I had misbehaved. Other times it was because we had something to show him. But mostly it was because my dad could fix anything broken. This statement meant when he came home, he would make it right, fix it, and make it work again.

In the context of Jeremiah 23:4-6 God was saying, "Yes, I see how my sheep are being mistreated and scattered. The shepherds are wicked and are taking advantage of them. But I am coming to put all things right again and to bring authority, peace, and prosperity. I will release justice and righteousness; I will nurture and feed my people. The shepherds I will bring will restore what has been broken. My sheep will live in peace and security, because My name is Jehovah-Tsidkenu, the Lord is Righteous, God-Who-Puts-Everything-Right!"

What a picture of the Ruler gift! Our Father will fix the injustice, repair the broken, and put everything back in right order. Once again we see the Father's heart displayed. Sovereign Authority, yes. Righteous Judge, yes. Nurturing Protector, yes. They will not live in panic or fear but will dwell in security because Jehovah-Tsidkenu is on the scene.

Remember the "I've got your back" characteristic of the Ruler? The fathering anointing? The "get it done" mentality? Enough said.

The Ark of the Covenant

The sixth piece of furniture in the Tabernacle was the Ark of the Covenant. Reflecting the Ruler gift, this golden box contained three items:

- The Ten Commandments—God's standard of righteousness and holiness.
- The Golden Pot of Manna—the Father Heart of God through provision
- Aaron's Rod—supernatural God-given appointment and authority

The Ten Commandments. There is no sliding scale of holiness or righteousness. It is all or nothing. This holy and righteous standard is met only in one place, the blood of Jesus. Here the Ruler must refuse to rely on his own ability to lead people and turn to full dependence on Christ alone. Only to the degree that he is submitted to God's law can he be a life-giver to those who follow him.

The Golden Pot of Manna. God's supernatural provision. This "bread" contained all of the nutrients that were needed to sustain life and to enrich and release fullness of life.

Aaron's rod. Only after the Ten Commandments and the Manna were present do we see Aaron's rod that budded, representing the sovereign appointment of God. As others rebelled against God's choice for the priesthood, God made it very clear to those in the camp that Aaron would stand before Him as priest. Just as Nehemiah and Aaron both stood in the face of opposition to God's sovereign call on their lives, you, too, Ruler must stand in order to release the Father's heart to the people. You will accomplish this by depending upon God alone to make clear His sovereign call and His position of authority for you. You must follow in the footsteps of Jesus, who saw that His Kingship was not a thing to be grasped. He laid it all aside for the glory of the Father. But as He entered back into heaven after the cross and resurrection, He was once again given the scepter of authority to rule the universe!

The message here for the Ruler is nurture and humility according to Micah 6:8: "to do justly, to love mercy, and to walk humbly with your God." Then God will release your sovereign appointment, the one thing you are called to build.

Ruler Stronghold and Root Iniquity: Predator Spirit and Exploitation of People

"Using people and loving the project, taking more than you give back, and 80% is good enough" are the marks of a predator spirit in the unrighteous Ruler. When not following the example of Jesus, his natural inclination is to get the job done regardless of who is wounded and exploited or who has to pay the price. Cutting corners and not quite completing a task before beginning the next one can leave others in the lurch to finish what he started. His unfulfilled promises can wound others and cause disillusionment or dissatisfaction. Such covenant-breaking can even empower a victim spirit in individuals who think there must be something wrong in them to expect more from the Ruler than he wishes to give.

Simply put, not moving in righteousness, not completing the job, and not fathering all paint the picture of a carnal Ruler. In his inability to comprehend the one thing he is destined to build, the carnal Ruler moves from project to project like Solomon, the frustrated king who died declaring, "All is vanity!"

We get the picture of what an unredeemed Ruler looks like, but now let's see how God wants to restore the Ruler gift to what He intended when He created him.

Time with Father

One cannot give away what he does not possess, and one becomes what he focuses on. The only way the Ruler can fulfill his destiny and discover that one thing, his sovereign appointment, is to gaze upon the beauty of the Lord and to seek Him in His temple. Psalm 27:4.

As Adam and God sat in the cool of the day, their conversation was not the important thing, or it would have been recorded. The significant matter is they spent time together, getting to know each other. Children spell love "TIME" and so does the Father. Fatherhood is caught, not taught. As the ruler spends time in Father's presence, he will know the one thing he is to do, learn how to give more than he takes, but, most importantly, he will grasp the holiness and righteousness of Jehovah-Tsidkenu. Gaining access to the finishing anointing of Jesus, he will grasp how to appropriate His blood to cleanse, renew, and empower, especially at the place he is ready to stop short and quit too soon. Only then will he develop the essential virtue of becoming a spiritual life-giver. As my friend Sylvia Gunter would say, "A chip off the ole block!"

Jesus as Ruler

Jesus revealed His gift of Ruler time and again as He ministered in the earth. He invested in the spirits of men who became spiritual giants, fathering them in the most excellent way. Always about the Father's business, Jesus personified the nurture of the Father. He revealed to us that the law of the Lord is not just a list of Ten Commandments or rules to follow, but the design of a loving Father's boundaries for His children.

He was born in Bethlehem, came out of Egypt, lived in Nazareth. All fulfillment of the Old Testament prophesies. 100%. He brought healing, deliverance and hope to many in Israel, not leaving one jot or title of prophecy unfulfilled.

Understanding His dominion over Creation, he caused a fish to pay Peter's tax and even cursed a fig tree because it did not bear fruit. When asked about the Father, He said, "When you have seen Me, you have seen the Father!"

Many opportunities presented themselves to create a network, bring social change, and even build His own kingdom.

But all of these were not His sovereign appointment.

Jesus knew and accomplished the 'one thing' He came to do. He redeemed the world.

But what happens, Ruler, when you have gone your limit? What happens when you cannot figure out which project is the 'one thing,' much less finish it? What do you do when nurturing comes hard, and you are tempted to cut corners or just quit?

Jesus saw that you had no finishing anointing, no heart for the broken, no way to live in the standard of holiness required. He met the challenge for you. He finished the task and opened the way for you to experience your victory. Ruler, He had your back.

The Last Words of Jesus on the Cross: "It is finished!"

Three of the Gospels record there was Darkness at the cross for three hours. This same Darkness, which covered the face of the deep before our God spoke "Light." was filled with evil, wickedness, and chaos. Jesus even spoke about an outer darkness in Matthew 25:30, where He said there would be weeping and gnashing of teeth. This was the Darkness at the cross.

The entire earth felt this Great Darkness as every demon in the earth realm, the heavenly realm, and the realm below came to this place. Every sin you or I have ever committed or will ever commit and every form of evil and demon in hell were all present in one location: Calvary.

One by one by one, they tormented Him. Adultery! Blasphemy! Little white lies! Some iniquities were so evil we do not even have a name for them. Some were so minor we might not even recognize them as sin. But they were all there.

Did He look to the past and see Pharaoh, Haman, and all the others? Did He look toward the future to see Hitler and all of the wars to be fought?

As He peered into this Darkness, did He see me? Did He see you? Did He see every temptation that would come against us or every time we would fail to measure up? Did He see every slip of the tongue, or every time we denied Him?

One by one by one, they came. And one by one by one He defeated them. Our Great Champion did not stop until the prince of Darkness himself showed up.

Can you imagine the taunting and the evil laughter as the devil rattled the keys of the kingdom in His face? Did he remind Jesus of the day in the wilderness when He was offered these keys for a cheap, easy price? Did he remind Him that He didn't have to really suffer all this pain, sorrow, and sacrifice?

Looking at the bigger picture, visualize what was happening simultaneously at the altar in the temple. The priest was preparing the Passover lamb, on display since 9:00 that morning, for the yearly sacrifice. At 3:00 in the afternoon, he lifted the knife to slice the lamb's throat so that its blood could flow freely upon the altar.

And just outside Jerusalem at 3:00 in the afternoon, on the altar of Eternity our Passover Lamb was facing the enemy of our souls, an enemy who could not be defeated by an animal sacrifice. He was an enemy who could only be defeated by the pure, spotless blood of the Lamb of God, slain from the foundation of the world.

As the priest in the temple shouted, "It is finished! The debt is paid in full for another year!" there went up another shout that echoed throughout all eternity.

"It is finished! The debt is paid in full forever!"

And my sin was stamped in red: PAID IN FULL!

Our Mighty Deliverer defeated His greatest enemy. Truth Himself had vanquished the father of lies. Light spoke and the Darkness scattered.

Hebrews tells us Jesus descended into hell following His death on the cross. Can you hear the shouts of the captives as Lord Sabbaoth, the Commander of the Angel Armies, clothed with all authority of heaven and earth, marched into hell and stated, "I'll take those keys now."

Chains began to break. Prison doors began to open. And He led the captives home. He had the keys.

Death? Hades? The grave? He had the keys!

Now all the kingdoms of the earth are His. He will build His Church, and the gates of hell will not prevail against it. He has the keys.

No bondage, no chains can bind His kids any longer. He has the keys.

Rulers, when you cannot finish your race, when you cannot complete the 'one thing,' look to Jesus. Bow your knee at the altar of the cross, and remember that He, and He alone, is the Author and the Finisher of your faith. You cannot, but He did.

He completed the one thing. He finished the course. Now, at last, His Kingdom has been released in the earth, because this magnificent Ruler completed the job. 100%.

And the Father was pleased to announce His sovereign appointment that established His Son's authority forever.

"Who being the brightness of His glory, and the express image of His person, and upholding all things by the word of His power, when He had by Himself purged our sins, sat down on the right hand of the Majesty on high… But to the Son He says: 'Your throne, O God, is forever and ever. A scepter of righteousness is the scepter of Your kingdom.'" Hebrews 1:3,8.

The Treasure of the Ruler

As world changers, Rulers, you finish what God has called you to do: build His Kingdom. And as you build, carrying out your sovereign commission, release spiritual blessings of the Father to the generations, making disciples of all nations.

The world is crying out for fathers and mothers in the faith. Ruler, as you spend time daily in the Garden to know your Father, you are equipped and appointed to release His Father Heart to a fatherless generation.

We see in you the capacity to finish the course, to run the race. Partnering with the Master Builder, you raise up and establish a structure made of living stones, who are the young men and women that you mentor. As you position imperfect, broken people for success, you bring them to spiritual maturity so they can shine and sparkle with the light of His glory.

With your authority over the predator spirit, you understand the nurture required to set the captives free because you are supernaturally life-giving.

So commission these sons and the daughters, these living stones, to mobilize the Kingdom in new ways. Let them stand on your shoulders to see farther and wider than you. This is the spiritual blessing they are hungry for. Ruler, show us the Father!

Chapter Eight
The Gift of Mercy

The gift Mercy is the paradox of the gifts. One minute Mercy is gazing upon the beauty of the Lord, savoring His presence and majesty. The next minute he is cutting off the head of a giant in passionate, holy savagery. To the Mercy gift, it is all the same: Worship. Whereas the Exhorter loves the dramatic, the Mercy gift loves the extreme.

Mercy Characteristics

- The Mercy has the potential to bring extravagant worship into everyday situations. His domain, his DNA, is worship.

- Everyone loves a Mercy. He rarely has enemies and enjoys many relationships. The wounded and broken feel safe with him. Even at soccer games or at the supermarket, hurting people will quickly bear their soul and pour out their deepest need to a Mercy. He can enter a room and immediately be drawn to the most rejected and needy. Listening intently, he feels the sorrow of these people on a deep level.

- Because the Mercy listens and feels the pain of others so deeply, he must have a few intimate friends who love him, are there for him, and do not demand from him. These relationships help keep him balanced.

- Very intuitive, he hears facts or data with his heart first. After filtering situations through his emotions, he then grasps it in his head. This is exactly the opposite of how the rest of the world processes information. Most Mercies tend to deal with situations slowly and out loud. Listening with his heart, he must circle around the issue verbally several times before feeling it is aligned in his spirit and then he can let it rest. When attempting to communicate this to others, many times he is misunderstood and criticized, or marginalized and ignored.

- Pleasing people drives the carnal Mercy. Therefore, he will say "Yes" to many things and allow others to invade his boundaries. However, once he becomes overwhelmed with so many commitments, he may look for an escape, make excuses for not showing up, and deal with the consequences later. This tendency gives the Mercy the appearance of being fickle, of being unable to keep commitments, and of being irresponsible. For the Mercy, this is classic denial.

- Denial for the Mercy comes in many forms. Life situations, expectations from others, crowds, noise, or even thoughts of the future can overwhelm him, causing him to "check out." He may do it with video games, with television or books, by living in "la la land," or by leaving the scene in some other way. After a while, most Mercies will come back to reality, be refreshed, and be ready to face the issues once more.

- During this checkout time, a Mercy is emotionally processing the situation, bringing himself into alignment, and deciding what needs to be done. When peace comes on the inside, then he can move forward. The sad truth is that some Mercies live in this state of denial forever, unable to come to terms with reality. They float along, dreaming of the day when things will be better. To some, the Mercy appears spacey, out of touch, or just plain weird.

- Competition is strong in a Mercy, yet not the kind of competition that wins a game or runs the fastest. Competition for a Mercy is on a much deeper level. It is competition to be the pick of the bunch, the cream of the crop, to be the one who is chosen first and who wants others to like him the best.

- The Mercy is prone to be indecisive because he doesn't want to make a choice between two opinions. For instance, it can be as simple as Sue wants Mexican food, and Sally wants Chinese. For the Mercy, it is not the choice of food. It is having to choose between Sue and Sally.

- His first response in decision-making is to match himself to the other person so that his decision will match the other person's need. Later he will process it, circle around it, and then know his own true response.

- Before the Mercy can really engage in a situation, he must connect emotionally and somehow become personally involved, even if it is only by learning one fact about the circumstances. For instance, in order to engage with a particular football or baseball team, he must know something personal about that team. He may know one of the players, the coaches, or the owners. This way, he emotionally connects and can become passionate about their season's wins or losses.

- The mercy was created to "be," to savor beauty, and to celebrate creation. Alone time is essential for him. People love him, and he loves people, and he needs to be with people. But there comes a time when he must seek out a quiet place, a place of order, where he can relish and appreciate life, existence, order, and beauty. Just to "be."

- Slow to transition from one place to the next, from one emotional state to another, the Mercy needs time. He wants to hold on to the last moments of a vacation, but he may begin to transition emotionally a couple of days before the vacation ends, preparing himself for the change. In a big, life-changing decision, he may appear to move too quickly. What others do not know is he has been transitioning for a while. He has been looking at all sides and playing out all the emotional scenarios in his mind weeks before the deadline. Once his decision is made, he seems to be swift and decisive. Cutting ties, he moves on. However, for the Mercy this process has not been quick at all. He has thought about it, felt the emotions of it, counted the cost of it long before the final decision.

- On the negative side, a Mercy can become an enabler who tolerates anything except intolerance, including emotional pain to himself. He justifies sin because of the presence of pain in others and takes up an offense for the people he is seeking to help.

- God created the Mercy gift for intimacy. The Mercy craves and needs physical contact. There is an appropriate way for this need to be met. However, in our culture it is difficult and often misunderstood, even by the Mercy. If a Mercy is unredeemed, his craving for intimacy and physical contact can lead to promiscuity and an immoral lifestyle. He looks for love in all the wrong places. Couple this with his driving desire to please people, and we see it often leads to abuse and victimization of the Mercy.

- But don't get the idea the Mercy gift is all about pain or being an easy target. Earmarked by passion and the extreme, he enjoys fun, likes to laugh a lot, and can be the life of the party. The flip side of this is he can be a ruthless warrior when the need arises, cutting off heads and taking no prisoners.

- The Mercy understands, recognizes, and longs for alignment, which means balance, order, for everything to be in the correct or appropriate relative positions. He yearns for the time when everything is in its place and working as designed. This longing is so intense at times he will state, "I long for Jesus to come back." Or "I long to be with Jesus." This is not a death wish. It is the longing for a time when all of creation comes back into Sabbath day alignment, when all of creation functions as it was designed to function.

Mercy Characteristics as Seen in Bible Personalities

Some Mercies in the Bible were John the disciple; David the king; Joshua the warrior. Looking at all three of these, we will see a pattern of worship and alignment.

John the Disciple

When the woman with the alabaster jar gave extravagant worship to Jesus, those closest to Him misunderstood and criticized her. They saw this act through their eyes of reason. She was a woman and the alabaster jar was very expensive. Showing this much emotion in public was embarrassing, and this expense was, after all, quite wasteful. But John, the disciple and Mercy gift, saw this woman's heart, not her act. While the others processed the scene with worldly wisdom and came to the logical conclusion, "The ointment should have been sold and the money given to the poor," John's account states, "The fragrance of the oil filled the house." I believe he, along with Jesus, savored the sweet aroma. The others missed this beautiful moment in time. But John did not, and neither did Jesus. They represent classic Mercy gift.

Early on, as the disciples followed Jesus, we can note several occasions when John wanted to be the best, the closest, and the most loved. He stood by, listening as his mother asked for her sons to have the honor of sitting at Jesus' right hand when He came into His glory.

John needed and sought intimacy with Jesus. He leaned on the breast of Jesus. Was he listening for His heartbeat? He longed to be Jesus' best friend. All the way through the book of John, we see him pushing closer and closer to Jesus. Jesus understood John and reached out to John to let him know he was in His inner circle.

Knowing the heart of the Mercy, one that is drawn to the wounded and listens with excellence, did Jesus confide in John? Jesus incarnated in all seven of the Romans 12 gifts. Did His Mercy heart and John's connect more closely than the other disciples? Maybe so. Many times he referred to himself as "the disciple whom Jesus loved." John was there for his best friend as Jesus was dying on the cross. And John was the only one whom Jesus addressed from the cross. Jesus trusted John and knew he would be there for Him, so He asked John to take care of His mother.

Three of the most intimate books of the Bible are the three Epistles of John. He was known throughout Asia Minor as the apostle of love, even in the face of severe persecution. His influence, his love for others, and his revelation of the Father's love helped shape early Christianity.

The authorities of the day attempted to kill him, but they could not. Instead, he was exiled to a lonely, barren rock called Patmos in the middle of the sea. But John was far from lonely. The heart and DNA of the Mercy gift is extravagant, creative worship. And worship he did. His worship was so intimate, so intense, that the heavens opened one day, and he was caught up into unrestrained, glorious worship in the throne room of the Lamb. John was truly invited to join the inner circle. With his own eyes and his own ears, he saw, experienced, and recorded the highest, most intimate worship of the universe—worship of the King of kings and Lord of lords—the worship of Jesus, his best friend.

Deep intimacy, true worship, and extreme passion all characterize the worship of John, the disciple whom Jesus loved.

Joshua

Many look at the Mercy gift as women who want to worship all of the time. Yep! Most of those women are Mercy gift. But there is much more to the Mercy than meets the eye. Try this description: ruthless, bloodthirsty warrior. Can we get much more extreme? Probably not. Yet Joshua, a classic Mercy, was chosen to lead the armies of Israel into the Promised Land.

Joshua knew his mighty God, Jehovah, intimately and well. What was Joshua's address? It was the Tent of Meeting with Moses. Even when Moses left, Joshua stayed in God's presence. Worship was his DNA.

Joshua had observed Jehovah's mighty right hand against the Egyptian chariots. Fighting alongside Lord Sabbaoth, the Commander of the Angel Armies, he had tasted sweet victory against the Amalekites. Giants in the land? Joshua's perception was the bigger they are, the harder they fall. Yes, Joshua knew Jehovah face to face.

The command rang out, "Go and take the land!" Joshua was ready with sword in hand. He took no prisoners; he killed them all.

And Jehovah knew this mighty warrior, Joshua. Jehovah knew Joshua would fight to the death for the honor of the God of Israel. Whereas the Prophet fights for justice, the Mercy fights for honor. God knew the fire of a warrior coursed through his veins. He knew because He had put it there.

Jehovah was aware of the issues in the heart of the Mercy. He knew the insecurity, the need for validation, and the drive to please people.

He understood the taunting spirit that caused this Mercy to second-guess, rethink, and question, "Did I really hear God?" Three times the Lord said to Joshua, "Be strong and courageous!"

Stepping into Moses' position as leader, Joshua would lead from his heart, but he wanted the heart of the people with him. This connection is a priority for leadership in the Mercy. As Joshua called the army together, they shouted, "We will follow you, just as we did

Moses." Sounds good to the ears, but did he have their hearts? I don't think so. They were still comparing Joshua to Moses. But God had his back.

As the priests, carrying the Ark, stepped into the Jordan River, it parted. Remember, the Mercy recognizes alignment and carries presence, bringing that alignment and presence into the present. Joshua knew how to align with The Presence represented by the Ark of the Covenant. Moses divided the Red Sea with his rod, but as Joshua aligned the people with the Ark of the Covenant, The Presence divided the Jordan. The Ark of the Covenant went first, representing a huge shift.

The Word states that on that day Jehovah exalted Joshua in the sight of the people, and they honored and revered him all the days of his life. He now had their hearts.

David

Savage warrior, extravagant worshiper, passionate lover— all three of these descriptions fit David to a "T." And all three caused problems in his life, either with God or with people. The Mercy gift is all or nothing. They do 'extreme' well.

Savage warrior. David ran to the giant, fighting for the honor of the God of Israel. Without stopping, he cut off Goliath's head and became the hero of the day. It seemed nothing stopped this wild, untamable, ferocious, young fighter. The women sang, "Saul killed his thousands, but David killed his ten thousands." Consequently, Saul hunted David until the day Saul died.

Extravagant worshiper. David danced before the Lord with such abandon, he flung off his clothes. Michal, his wife, saw and criticized him. From that day on, she was barren. Could it be they were never intimate again?

Passionate lover. This time, with Bathsheba, God was displeased with David. His desire for immediate physical fulfillment and passion cost David the life of his son. But you just gotta love David. He was quick to repent, and Psalm 51 has become the guideline for all of us as we see his brokenness. His recognition of the depth of his sin was not the lust for Bathsheba or even the murder of Uriah, although both were sinful and grievous to the Lord. The realization that he had sinned against God, his most intimate Friend, broke David's heart and brought such anguish and repentance.

Other Mercy characteristics in David, some not so honorable, include his propensity to hold bitterness against those who wounded him. As King David was leaving the city after Absalom had crowned himself king, Shimei, descendent of Saul, began cursing and throwing stones at him. Of course, his men wanted to take care of him in a flash, but David stopped them.

Later after Absalom died and David was back in Jerusalem as king, Shimei came and asked if he had permission to move back into town. King David had the choice to kill him, refuse him, or let it go. This Mercy gift king smiled and said, "Sure, come on back, Shimei."

Now let me explain what is happening in David's heart. I know this scenario well, unfortunately. The Mercy wants to show kindness to those around him so others will be impressed with his benevolence and honor him. He wants to please people. "Oh, look how wonderful he is, so forgiving and kind." That statement is music to the ears of a Mercy.

But inside he is saying, "You hurt me, but you will never know it. Now I will pick up and carry a stone of bitterness in my heart forever against you. Some day I'll have my revenge."

How do I know David did this? It is a common stronghold for the Mercy, as is shown in one of David's last requests from his deathbed. In commissioning Solomon as the next king, he spoke to him about the plans for the temple, about how to manage the kingdom, and about a few personal desires. He told Solomon, "And remember Shimei and what he did to me when I had to leave Jerusalem. Make him pay." 1 Kings 2:9 (The Message). David had carried this bitterness to his death. Being loyal to his father, Ruler Solomon took care of Shimei shortly after he was crowned king. David came off still looking like the kind, benevolent king, which in reality he was, while loyal ruler, Solomon, took care of the revenge.

Another caution for all Mercies is the sin of presumption. Intuitively understanding right alignment, yet moving in his own instinct without consulting the Lord, he risks the sin of presumption. David's desire for alignment, coupled with his DNA of worship, caused him to long for the Ark of the Covenant to be the central focus for the nation of Israel. However, moving in the wrong time or the wrong way, although it is the right thing, can have devastating results. David's first attempt to bring up the Ark ended in disaster. The Ark faltered, a man died, and the celebration came to a sudden halt. It would be a while before the Ark would enter the city. David had learned the hard way that it had to be God's way in God's time with God's priests.

Recently, while reading the "River Walk" blog, a post called "The King of Bandits"[4] caught my attention. I was fascinated by yet another glimpse at David's ability to lead his army. In pondering this perspective, I saw a deeper aspect of David as a Mercy gift. His mighty men were not mighty men at all when he chose them. They were "men who were in trouble or in debt or who were just discontented." 2 Samuel 22. These were brutal, fierce, violent, bloodthirsty men looking for a fight. Actually, David didn't choose them. They chose David. Remember, a Mercy gift is all about the heart, the broken and wounded. David, the giant-killing rebel, was not so much better than they were. He knew it, and they knew it. But David had something they didn't have—a deep intimate relationship with Jehovah-Rohe, his Shepherd.

David was a man after God's heart, and he carried God's heart for these men. He ate, drank, and slept in tents with them, listening to their fearless feats and their deepest sorrows. After years of fighting together they became his Mighty Men. We are told of their awesome exploits. They were lion killers, giant killers, and army killers.

What changed this ragtag group of cutthroats into mighty men of distinction, commanders of thousands? Time with David. David had won their hearts because he listened to them. He envisioned how they could shift from common thieves to men of valor. He imparted to them a heart of mercy which wars for honor, not justice, fame, or treasure. That kind of loyalty could not be bought. It was earned hiding together in the Judean wilderness running from Saul and fighting for their lives.

These ruffians were loyal to David because they honored and loved him. Upon hearing that David longed for a drink of water from the gate of Bethlehem, they risked their lives, broke through enemy lines, and fought their way back to satisfy their beloved Captain's thirst.

True to his character, David saw how precious this gift of water was, as precious as the blood of the men who brought it to him. It was holy. He poured it out to the Lord as an offering, honoring them, and calling them "The Three," who were set apart from all others. David's Mighty Men were the fruit of David's Mercy heart.

David, awesome king, passionate worshiper, holy savage, is known today as the man after God's own heart.

Mercy's Foundational Principle: Fulfillment

"Nothing broken, nothing missing" is one way of explaining the fulfillment so craved by the Mercy. We were all created spirit, soul, and body, in that order. Only as the spirit leads the way can a Mercy find the alignment he so desires. Being sensitive in all three areas, he can sense when others, the atmosphere, or his environment is out of order. This disorder causes discomfort or dissatisfaction in his spirit. By staying in tune with the Holy Spirit and being connected to Him, he can bring himself, others, and even his environment into this divine alignment.

As the Mercy stays in personal alignment, spirit leading the way, he will discover appropriate ways to be fulfilled in his soul and body.

Mercy's Birthright: Blessing of Presence

The Mercy's call is to come into Jehovah's presence for a transfer of His holiness much like a battery being recharged. Then he is to go back out and live in the earth to release His glory, erasing the line between our everyday lives and what we would consider holy or religious. This blessing of presence allows him to live in dominion over sin and unholy circumstances and to release God's holiness into all spheres of culture.

Romans 12:1 tells us to present our bodies as a living sacrifice because this is our reasonable worship. This verse especially applies to the Mercy gift. Because his domain is worship, it is his DNA to worship wherever he is, whether at Wal-Mart or at a gathering of the Church. Cleaning the floor, putting in a good day's work, or taking a casserole to a neighbor are all worship for the Mercy. Wherever he is at the moment becomes a place to release God's holiness, His goodness, and His love. This is perhaps why the brokenhearted are so drawn to the Mercy. He has the capacity to bring them into the only Presence who can truly heal their broken heart.

Seventh Day of Creation

Genesis 2:1-3 "Thus the heavens and the earth, and all the host of them, were finished. ²And on the seventh day God ended His work which He had done, and He rested on the seventh day from all His work which He had done. ³Then God blessed the seventh day and sanctified it, because in it He rested from all His work which God had created and made."

The work was finished. There was nothing left to do but savor, enjoy, contemplate, absorb, rest, and bask in the glow of a job well done!

And God did just that. He celebrated with Adam and Eve. All was beautiful, perfect, and in divine alignment. Everything in creation functioned as it was designed to function, including the man. The trees produced fruit, the birds flitted and sang, the flowers bloomed, and the man joyfully visited and communed with his Father, his Creator.

Adam was a Mercy gift.

All was as it should be. Nothing missing, nothing broken. Perfect rest.

The complete fulfillment of God's design was the seventh day. This was His finest day, His best idea, His long-desired dream. God and His friends living together in relationship, community, and oneness with each other. It was so wonderful for our Father/Creator, He could not hold back His blessing. He blessed this magnificent day and set it apart as holy. God sanctified time as the first created thing to be made holy.

You too, Mercy, are called to sanctify time, bless it, and release His holy presence into it. You move at the slowest pace. While others analyze, you are called to contemplate, savor, and enjoy beauty. You absorb truths about the nature of God that will not reach your mind. You see His fingerprints in the smallest detail that others miss.

Intuitively understanding and hungering for perfect alignment, you know there can be no rest without it.

Just as First Fruits celebration is strategic for the Prophet, Sabbath is essential for you, Mercy. An hour here and a minute there will not "get it" for you. Setting aside a day, a full Sabbath, will shift and change your life. If you say, "I'm too busy to take a full day's Sabbath," the Jews would say to you, "So you are busier than God?"

After the fall, there were cherubim placed at the gate of the garden with fiery swords. Ever since that day, "Adam" (all mankind) has been seeking a way back to this perfect alignment.

Side note: There are curses and blessings on time. October 31 is another day in the calendar of God. He was there first. But men have the authority to bless or curse land and time according to their words, lifestyle, and practices. Halloween, because of continued occult worship, has defiled this day, this time. The Mercy gift has the anointing to bring intentional, extravagant, holy worship to this time to redeem and sanctify it.

Selah! Thank You, Father, for men like James Nesbit, Mercy gift, and others who have understood this principle and are intentionally releasing extraordinary worship on this day across our nation!

Jehovah-Shammah

As Ezekiel prophesied the restoration of the temple and described the city not made with hands, he declared Jehovah-Shammah—The Lord is Present, The Lord is There. No longer would they search and fail to find Him. He would be present in His temple, His city, and His people. No longer would there be a separation between their ordinary, everyday lives and their religious or holy times with the Lord. His presence would permeate the whole earth. Until that day of complete restoration comes, every Christian carries a measure of His presence.

The Lord is there. The Lord is present. He is present there. There in the highest adoration of a choir singing on resurrection morning. There in the dirtiest slum of Bangladesh. He is there.

His Spirit hovered over darkness and chaos in the beginning. He was drawn to this darkness. It was offensive to Him and all that He is. He spoke. The darkness scattered. Light and alignment came.

You, Mercy, carry that portion of the Creator in you. You are drawn to brokenness and darkness. You long for alignment and light. And you intuitively know it is His presence that is necessary to shift it.

There is a time to soak in His presence, savor His beauty, and worship in His Holy place. But there is a time to come out and touch the unclean, pray for the broken, and embrace the sick and wounded. The Lord is there in His holy sanctuary, and He is there in the everyday lives of humanity. You are charged to reflect Jehovah-Shammah, the Light of His Presence, to a dark and hurting world.

The Mercy Seat

The Mercy Seat, the burning fire of His holiness residing in the earth, was a place of intimacy and worship. Here the visible glory of God rested.

It was difficult for our holy God to find a way to dwell in a tangible place. After all, He said, "Heaven is my throne, earth is my footstool." How could a holy God dwell in an unholy world and not consume it? In His love and concern for us, He placed barriers between Himself and men. Not because He desired it, but because we required it. In the Tabernacle the first barrier was the outer court, then the inner court, and finally the veil. Embroidered on the veil as a reminder of the fall were two cherubim with flaming swords. We see them once again, hovering over the Mercy Seat and protecting us from His consuming, burning holiness.

Only once a year did the high priest have access to this inner room, and then only with the blood of the Passover lamb. Jesus opened the way for us all to go into this Holy Place, into His very presence without being annihilated, burned up, or consumed.

Mercy, you seem to have the easiest access to go into this Holy Place and bring others with you. This is exquisitely your job to usher them in by your worship. However, your job is not just to take others in, but to bring out what you find there.

You go in, not because of necessity or requirement, but out of desire. The intimacy you find fulfills the yearning for the alignment that was lost to the first Adam. Only here can you find the fulfillment, peace, and strength your spirit requires to grow big enough to lead your soul and body. This is where you establish your steadfast relationship with the Lord. This is where you become saturated with His presence. And from here you can carry this blessing of His presence into your everyday life in the earth.

Our culture has attempted to remove His presence, but you are called to lead the way to bring it back. You are designed to be fully functional in the human world while at the same time dwelling in the presence of God. You lead the way, bringing His presence by simply being there. You have the essence to do that.

Mercy Stronghold and Root Iniquity: Self-Gratification, Bitterness, and Pleasing Self and Others

Self-gratification is the driving desire to be satisfied spirit, soul, and body, regardless of the cost. Mercy gift can be lost in that constant thirst to find the ultimate satisfaction. Unless he finds it spiritually in the Lord, he will be searching to find it in his soul or body. This "soul searching" can empower a spirit of jealousy, addiction, lust for position, or immorality. To the carnal Mercy, it is about feeling good, pleasing self, and others. When others cannot or will not meet the Mercy's expectations, he moves into the iniquitous pattern of bitterness. If fulfillment is not found in God's presence, the Mercy will continue to search in three areas.

Spirit. The Mercy's domain is worship, and he will worship. The question is "At what altar will he worship?" He may bow down to unholy altars of the occult. Spiritually intuitive, he realizes this darkness is real, and his spirit seeks the power and authority that is deceptively promised there. The lust for more ends in disillusionment, not fulfillment.

Soul. Yielding to a spirit of stubbornness and competition, whether in business, sports, or relationships, the Mercy strives to be the best friend, the top executive, the most desired athletic hero. Empowered by a spirit of jealousy, he judges God, accusing Him of allowing someone else to have the position or blessing that should have been his. This judgmental attitude or jealousy leads to increased bitterness and anguish in his soul.

Body. Sensual desires and physical contact drive many Mercies to an immoral lifestyle. Aching for touch and intimacy, the carnal Mercy looks for love in all the wrong places and moves from one physical relationship to the next. Seeking pleasure and gratification rather than the discipline of seeking God and His presence can also empower an addictive spirit. Such addiction can include drugs, alcohol, and gambling to name a few.

A people-pleaser, the unredeemed Mercy will embrace impurity and compromise in order to keep from offending anyone. He will tolerate anything but intolerance and accuse others of being insensitive or cruel if they attempt to address any sin issue. Feeling a false sense of responsibility, he may embrace guilt because someone's heart was not healed. He feels if he had been a better counselor, things would have gone better. Defaulting to feelings of guilt can lead to a victim spirit for the Mercy.

Although he seems to have very few enemies, he is quite sensitive to rejection and can be easily wounded. The pain of rejection is as deep as his need for intimacy. Rejection leads the carnal Mercy to build a wall against intimacy and hold on to bitterness. Although others may never know he has been wounded, he will make an inward vow, "I will close my heart to this person. I will continue to be kind on the surface, but I will never let them back into my heart for fear they will only hurt me again." He then picks up a stone of bitterness against them.

This iniquitous pattern can become so normal, he does not realize what is happening until he has built a wall so high he is trapped inside a prison of bitterness, jealousy, and revenge. This wall of offense is, in reality, against God Himself. David said, "Against You and You only have I sinned." Unable to go around it, through it, over it or under it, he cannot advance without the blood of Jesus. Only He can break through these thick prison walls and set the captives free.

Time with Father

"Choose the discipline of time with Father to find fulfillment in Him alone." That is such a Prophet statement. To put that into Mercy language, it means, "Stop! Ponder! Enjoy creation and beauty. Savor and meditate on His glory and majesty. As you carve small moments of time to be still, your heart will begin to yearn for more."

These moments turn into minutes and hours of learning to "be" in His presence. Not for what you can get or to hear your next assignment, but simply to "Selah", pause and reflect. In this atmosphere your battery becomes recharged, not with a "to do" list but with His joy, His love, and His excitement for His creation. His glory is transferred to your spirit. This is fulfillment. The more time you spend there, the larger your spirit grows in its capacity to hold more and more of Him. The closer you come to Him, the more intimacy you share. The battle to please others becomes less and less difficult because you are more concerned with honoring your Best Friend Jesus and making Him known.

We become what we gaze upon. Gaze upon His beauty, His majesty, His purity, His holiness, and His love. Then purity and holiness become a lifestyle. Celebrate your addictive spirit, because you are addicted to His presence, His glory, and His greatness.

Are we called to war like Joshua and David? Yes! Wars are won one battle at a time. Our first battle is to take the land inside our own heart.

As a Mercy, we fight on three levels. He has given us excellent weapons designed for these specific battles. Attempting to win the physical battle first, we constantly speak to ourselves, "I'm not going to do that any more!" knowing all the while we will do it again. That is the nature of the addictive spirit, and that is a victory we will not win on this playing field. Therefore, we must learn to be strategic in our warfare, allowing our spirit to lead an offensive attack. Otherwise, we will always be on the defensive, losing many battles in our body and soul.

The first battle must be won in our spirit. As we spend time in His presence and allow our spirits to grow big, our hearts begin to appreciate and meditate on God's Word. We are called to worship Him in spirit and in truth. We soar in the spirit, but His truth keeps us on target and grounded. We need both. As the plumb line of truth goes deeper into our spirit, we will live with wisdom in all the other battles. The truth sets us free, free to live in purity in our soul and in our body.

As we grow stronger in our spirit, we face strong battles in our soul. Holding on to the victory won in our spirit is the key to winning the battle in our soul. The soul is the location of the drive to please people, always be the first or the best, and bitter stronghold of jealousy. The playing fields for this battle are relationships, success and failures, and accomplishments. We want to be the best friend, the most successful salesman, musician, or artist, the fastest runner. We want the highest grade point average, or the accolades of the masses. When someone else gets the prize, or exceeds us in their success, we are angry, move in jealousy, and spit out accusation that this blessing should have been ours. This battle is about choice. The Word tells us to take on the mind of Christ for a pure thought life. This scripture in context is talking about choices Jesus made. He was King of the Universe, and He had all authority and glory. He chose us, not the glory. He chose us, not the authority. He chose us, not the fame. This is where we make our choice. We choose Him, not the glory, not the authority, not the fame.

As our spirit leads and our soul comes into submission, we then have the wisdom and confidence to stand against the battle in the physical realm. The Lord designed the Mercy for physical contact. Finding appropriate ways to live in this realm might be difficult, but it is not impossible. We are already armed spiritually with the plumb line of truth and wisdom. That wisdom will guide us into pure and holy choices.

As a homeschool mom, most mornings we would put on our spiritual armor, taking up the belt of truth. Weight lifters wear wide belts around their waists to give them strength abdominally. Does this belt give them more muscle mass? No, it supports the muscles already there and gives an extra measure of strength to lift heavy weight without injury. That is what knowing God's Word does for us. As temptation comes, our belt of truth gives us added strength to say "No" and to guide us into His path of righteousness.

The bottom line is that time with Father is the only way to find the fulfillment so needed by the Mercy to make the right choices.

Kind, compassionate Mercy, what happens to you when you have not made the right choices? You feel defeated, unable to get yourself back up. You find you are more broken than those who come to you for help. You have built walls inside your heart until they have become a prison made of anger, bitterness, and loneliness. You have blocked out the only intimacy that will bring the fulfillment you so desperately crave. Our fierce, passionate warrior Jesus was willing to move heaven and earth for you. He breaks down prison walls and sets captives free. He made a way for you, prodigal, to come home.

Jesus as Mercy

Submitting to His Father in spirit, soul, and body, Jesus lived in total fulfillment and alignment. Moved by compassion and drawn to the brokenhearted, He healed the sick, cleansed the lepers, and set the captives free. He raised the dead, giving little boys back to their mamas. Dining with all levels of society, lepers, rulers, and Pharisees, Jesus was Mercy gift in its highest form.

Refusing to live in competition, He could have out-shined them all. He was the best, He could do it better, but He never grasped for recognition. He really was the King of the Jews, but they never saw it. He really could have come down off the cross, but He didn't. Never seeking the approval of men, Jesus received validation from His Father alone.

Time with His Father was His priority and the strength of His life. He knew when to pull aside alone with His Father, talking to Him face to face. But he also knew when to come out of the quiet place, move among the noisy crowds, touching people and changing lives. Jesus was present and brought His Father's presence everywhere He went.

Jesus brought full alignment, which means to put into correct or appropriate position, by fulfilling every prophecy and breaking every curse. The life, death, and resurrection of Jesus would bring all creation back into supernatural alignment with the original design. Total reconciliation would now be possible with the Father, so the descendents of the first Adam could enter the Garden and enjoy relationship with Him again.

Because Sabbath is so strategic to the Mercy, the Lord of the Sabbath would unlock the gate of the Great Sabbath, the promised rest of Hebrews 4:1. Yes, Jesus knew the gift of Mercy well.

The Last Words of Jesus on the Cross: "Father, into Your hands I commit My spirit."

Jesus had never been separated from His Father. From the beginning of time itself, He had been intimate, One with Him. They were the Father, the Son, the Holy Spirit, the Three in One. Yet, today was different. All the angels, principalities, powers, and even the morning stars held their breath as the drama of Calvary transpired before all of creation.

Can you imagine the thoughts or conversation of the angelic army as they stood poised, swords drawn, keeping their eyes focused on the Father's face? At any moment He could give the signal and they would rush into the fray—rush to end this agony they were forced to watch unfold on a barren, forsaken hill aptly named the Skull. But the sign did not come, and the drama proceeded.

Perhaps they remembered how they were astounded as the great hand of Jehovah God reached into the deep and pulled out the dry land. Or perhaps they recalled how in awed stillness they watched as He blew His breath, His very own Ruach Spirit, into the man he had made. Time and again, He had parted the seas, stopped the sun, and released the angelic armies to fight for His people.

But today was unlike any day before. This was His only Son, and today was the day He would die. On the day He was born, the heavens burst into song, unable to contain the Father's joy. On the day He was baptized, the heavens thundered with His voice. But today on the day He was to die, the heavens were brass, and the Father was silent.

Quiet but alert, they continued to watch the Father's tear-streaked face as it expressed the pain of His heart. They had seen this look once before, on the day Adam left the garden. And now they watched His face again for the signal that never came.

The signal did not come, but the Darkness did. In hushed silence, they watched as their noble King continued to fulfill His covenant destiny alone, facing His enemy, the Prince of Darkness himself. They heard the jeers, the evil laughter, the taunting. Yet Jesus never flinched, nor turned His head, but continued on. They would have brought Him water, helped Him breathe, and even stopped the pain, but that was not to be.

Did they gasp as the earth began to tremble and shake free from the death and curse of all the ages? Were they astounded as they watched redemption, through the power of the blood of the Passover Lamb of God, begin to loosen the chains that had held creation bound since the fall? Did they remember when the Lamb was slain on the day Jehovah created light? Did they realize 'this' was 'that'?

The Gift of Mercy

It was almost over. But wait! There was one more piece to this drama that was yet to be played out. He had one last chain to break, one final lock to open, one final prison wall to destroy.

He had done the work, finished the task, and the price had been paid in full. All of this was required by His Father. The priests and Pharisees had plotted His death. Judas had betrayed Him. Pilate had released Him to die. Soldiers had beaten Him. Peter had left Him. Obedient to the end, He had vanquished His Father's every adversary.

The deeper the intimacy, the deeper the wound of rejection. Jesus realized ultimately all of this came from His Father. Asking if there could be another way, for the first time in all eternity He heard His Father say "No." The pain, the betrayal, and the shame, all had come from His Father's hand.

This Mercy gift Savior had one more choice to make. He could choose to reach down, pick up a stone of bitterness, and build a wall against intimacy with His Father. As He hung in this dark place, there was no evidence His Father still loved Him. There was no evidence to disprove He was forsaken. But our Great Champion reached down deeper still to remember there is always a bigger picture. "When you cannot see His face, trust His character. He is good."

His choice was made. He chose you, Mercy. He would not build a wall of offense. He would keep His heart open and His face toward His Father. One last time He pushed against the nails in His feet to gasp His final breath. Purposefully turning His face toward His Father, He whispered, "Father, into Your hands I commit My spirit." I am coming home!

This majestic King, this royal High Priest, walked into the Holy of Holies of heaven with His head held high, carrying His own precious blood. All of heaven trembled as the veil ripped before Him, the flaming swords of the Cherubim parted, and He poured His own holy sacrifice on the Mercy Seat.

And the Father? His tears gone, beaming with pride and joy, He had waited for this moment since the beginning, since the Fall.

With outstretched arms He ran, embracing His Son and shouting, "Well done! My Son. Welcome home! Bring the robe and put it on His shoulders! Bring the crown. Bring the scepter. My Son has come home!"

The Angelic host? There was so much celebration in heaven, it caused the earth to shake. Their King had returned to His glory, His authority, and His power. The curse was broken, resurrection and restoration were on the way!

Holy! Holy! Holy! Their song rang out through the ages as they glimpsed yet another depth of His holiness and His greatness. Oh! How they worshiped!

Hebrews 1 describes this scene in heaven. "Who being the brightness of His glory and the express image of His person, and upholding all things by the word of His power, when He had by Himself purged our sins, sat down at the right hand of the Majesty on high."

In the temple in Jerusalem, according to the writings of Josephus, another scene was unfolding. Suddenly, the thick veil with the cherubim embroidered on it ripped from top to bottom. A mighty wind rushed from the Holy of Holies, and the light of the huge Menorah was blown out. The bronze doors of the temple, which normally took several men to move, flung wide open by themselves. He went in as the Passover Lamb, but He came roaring out as the Lion of the tribe of Judah!

No longer would Jehovah God have to be separated by barriers from His children. The veil was torn, the flaming swords parted, and the way was opened into His presence. The Second Adam opened the way for the first Adam, the prodigal, to come back into the garden. His Son, Jesus, opened the door to the Great Sabbath rest for all of mankind. The way back for perfect communion with our Father-Creator. The way back for perfect alignment of all of Creation.

Mercy, He shattered your bitter prison walls and made a way back for you. When you could not, He did!

The Treasure of the Mercy

The curtain was torn for a purpose, to allow us to go in and experience His pure and holy mercy, cleansing us and making us whole. But you, Mercy, understand there is more. Jehovah-Shammah, His presence flows out to fill the earth with life, joy, peace, and kindness.

You have eyes to see His face everywhere you turn, whether in the beauty of nature or the soulful eyes of a hungry child. Both touch you so deeply because you carry His Mercy heart of passion to right the wrong, to embrace His children, and to father the fatherless. Entering in and out of the Holy of Holies so easily, you have the high privilege to take others into that place of healing, joy, and peace with you. But greater still is bringing His presence out into our everyday world, touching the lives of those around us with His joy and peace as we work, shop at the local Wal-Mart, and simply live our daily lives. This is the high call of the Mercy.

Each of the gifts has a specific anointing and moves in a note of music all its own. Releasing your sound as the first violin of the orchestra, you, Mercy, bring all the other gifts into alignment, positioning them to release their best sounds, brightest colors, closest harmonies, and most creative expressions of worship. Seeing how each has a place and how they all fit together gives the world a better glimpse of the many colored, multi-faceted wisdom of God displayed in His Church as we blend in unity.

You may enter into the Holy of Holies as a lamb, but you come out as a Mighty Warrior! Ride forth in victory to make His great name known to the nations. Release the roar of the Lion of Judah in the earth. Teach us all to war with holy passion and full obedience, becoming holy savages for the honor of our God.

Chapter Nine
So What?

What would a glimpse of the Church look like if we all moved fully in our grace gift?

Jesus.

He is a picture of all the gifts functioning together in one person.

Each grace gift brings an important portion, and without each one we are all incomplete. As we mature in His grace, we can function in all the gifts because we are commanded to be like Him. Even a Mercy, when living in His grace, can actually see the black and white of sin and with great trepidation confront it like a Prophet. Of course, it may take him an hour or two to do so. And the Exhorter can learn to listen to the quiet Teacher, when after pondering, she rises up to speak. However, essentially we will still see the world through our specific color or grace gift and respond in our hearts according to that paradigm.

The all-wise God of the Universe is the fullness of Light with seven visible, distinct colors. Created to reflect Him in all of His glory and all of His colors, we as the Church must come to maturity by living in our identity and giving grace to others. By doing so, we will see His Kingdom come in fullness on Earth.

But so what? What does that look like on Monday morning? We carry the presence of God into the market place as we live in the chaos of the world. As a nurse, in critical situations, I could pray and expect wisdom from the Ancient of Days. In economic situations, Christians become models of integrity, looking for resourceful ways to meet the needs of those around them. We display His goodness and love whether as a schoolteacher, bank president, or homemaker. He will design situations for us to display His character, manifested through our grace gifts. Romans 12 states, "Having then gifts differing according to the grace that is given to us, let us use them: if prophecy, let us prophesy in proportion to our faith; [7]or ministry, let us use it in our ministering; he who teaches, in teaching; [8]he who exhorts, in exhortation; he who gives, with liberality; he who leads, with diligence; he who shows mercy, with cheerfulness."

Giving Grace to All

We serve a God of grace. Grace is the facet of God's love that covers and protects. Some words that better define this grace are courtesy, decency, good manners, politeness, honor, and respect. Don't we all want to receive this grace from God? Don't we all want to receive this grace from others? We have discussed God's design for His children. My prayer is you will understand yourself better and will have new eyes to see others around you. But seeing is not enough. The only way for the world to know that He came will be for His Body to live in unity with Him and with each other. We as His children learn to embrace each other in his own uniqueness and to appreciate each other's anointing as a compliment to our own.

The one aspect of the fruit of the Spirit most often ignored seems to be kindness. Kindness expressed through grace. Jesus was kind. His kindness brings us to repentance. His kindness is expressed through courtesy, good manners, politeness, and respect—through grace.

As I've written about each of the grace gifts, I've come to better understand how to love and honor the Lord by extending this type of grace to my friends and to others. Although there are untold

So What?

numbers of ways to express love, here are some of my suggestions as to how to show grace to each grace gift:

- The Prophet—Appreciate his vision, recognize it, and watch for lane changes without signals. When he does this, give him grace.

- The Servant—Notice and value his contribution. When he has said "Yes" to everything, don't add to his list. Help him get it done. Give him grace.

- The Teacher—Honor the truth he brings. Verbally express your appreciation of his wisdom, research, and depth. If you need help from others with a project, don't ask the Teacher to ask them, do it yourself. Give him grace.

- The Exhorter—Show up and enjoy his party! When you see he needs to come away from people and spend time with God, don't rain on his parade. Pray for him and give him grace.

- The Giver—Look past the gift. See the thought and observation that went into it. Value the Giver, not the gift. When you need a commitment from him, be specific, explain why you need it and its importance to you. Give him options and never assume what he will do. Give him grace.

- The Ruler—Look past the project he is building and appreciate his intent, his plan, and his heart. When your agenda clashes with his, communicate the "why" and give him time to form another plan, which includes your agenda. Give him grace.

- The Mercy—Listen past the multitude of words as he processes the idea verbally, circling and circling until he nails it. When you hear the process begin, don't roll your eyes and write him off. Instead, listen and champion his voice. Give him grace.

The Orchestra

Without you, I am incomplete. There is no harmony with only one part. We must have other sounds, other notes in the chord, to be complete. There can be no orchestra with only a piano. The oboe, the flute, the drums, the strings, and the woodwinds are all integral parts of the whole.

Following the same conductor, the Holy Spirit, we will know when to play softly or build to fortissimo! Just because there is only one cymbal crash in the Star-Spangled Banner does not mean it can be played without cymbals. That crash at the end puts us over the top. Our part is important. With only one flute, the music is beautiful but not extraordinary. Our God is after the extraordinary!

The Prophet brings vision; the Servant, atmosphere; the Teacher, the plumb line of truth; the Exhorter, hope and light; the Giver, birth, value, and provision; the Ruler, the plan and Father's heart; the Mercy, His manifest presence and alignment of all the gifts. Like the first violin of the orchestra, this alignment prepares us as the Church to move in harmony and function in the earth as one. Different instruments, different harmonies, but together we are the Hallelujah Chorus.

As this miracle happens, the prayer of the Lord in John 17 is released to a hungry world. "Father, make them one, as You and I are one." We become one in purpose, each with our own assignment and anointing, moving together in unity that the world may know He came.

The Church, the Season, the Change

The season of the Church has changed. The Kingdom is here; it is coming. The components, His gifts, are in position. We need to look at all the gifts to see how their anointing fits into the equation.

- The five-fold gifts in Ephesians 4 are given to the Church to teach and equip all of the Body to come into maturity and ministry.
- The manifestation gifts of the Holy Spirit in I Corinthians 12, like the anointing oil, help us flow supernaturally as we come together or as we minister to others.
- The revelation of the Romans 12 gifts gives identity to the individual believer and increases our unity of purpose.

In this new season, the enemy is targeting the unity of the Church through jealousy, territorialism, and competition, but we are all on the same team. By being aware of his tactics, we can come in the opposite spirit to enforce the victory Jesus already won for us on the Cross.

These strongholds will be defeated person-to-person, church-to-church, and region-to-region, as we see alignment come in the Church as a whole. Knowing our place, our gift, and our assignment causes us to come into supernatural alignment so we can release synergistic power through the blood of Jesus.

The enemy knows this unity and alignment is the final straw for him, and he is unleashing all he has to prevent this from happening. It will take all the gifts—the governmental gifts, the Holy Spirit manifestation gifts, and the grace gifts, moving in synergy with one another, to defeat Him. But never forget, we cannot progress in our anointing without the blood of Jesus applied to each battle.

Prayer

Lord, bring us into the fullness of our identity in You. Cause us to grow up and reach maturity so we can embrace each other and Your holiness to reveal to the world what a marvelous Savior and King You really are. Lord, make us one that the world may know ...

Appendix A
Lists of Sevens

Throughout the Bible there are numerous lists of "sevens." Below are just a few of these. As we compare the lists, we begin to see similarities in how the numbers correspond to each other.

- The Grace Gifts of Romans 12:6-8
- The Seven Days of Creation, Genesis 1:1-2:3
- God's promise to Abraham, Genesis 12:1-3
- Furniture in the Tabernacle, Exodus 25
- Feasts of the Israelites
    - Passover
    - Unleavened Bread
    - First Fruits
    - Pentecost
    - Trumpets
    - Atonement
    - Tabernacles
- Compound names of Jehovah
    - Jehovah-Jireh, the Lord who Provides, Genesis 22:14
    - Jehovah-Rapha, the Lord who Heals, Exodus 15:22-26
    - Jehovah-Nissi, the Lord our Banner, Exodus 17:14-16
    - Jehovah-Shalom, the Lord our Peace, Judges 6:11-24
    - Jehovah-Rohe, the Lord my Shepherd, Psalm 23:1
    - Jehovah-Tsidkenu, the Lord our Righteousness, Jeremiah 23:6

- Jehovah-Shammah, the Lord who is Present, Ezekiel 48:35
- Miracles of Elijah beginning in 1 Kings 17:1
- Descriptions of God in Psalm 18:2
- Voices of God in Psalm 29
- Abominations of Proverbs 6:16-19
- Petitions in the Lord's Prayer, Matthew 6:9
- Parables of Matthew 13
- Woes of Matthew 23
- The Works of Christ, Luke 7:21-23
- Miracles of Christ in the Gospel of John
- Last words of Christ on the Cross
- The Christian Armor from Ephesians 6:14-18
- Qualities of Wisdom in James 3:17
- Churches in Revelation 2-3
- Song to the Lamb in Rev. 5:12 and to the Father in Rev. 7:12
- And more

List of Resources

Here are other books and resources I recommend to help with a deeper understanding of the Romans 12 gifts:

The Father's Business (www.thefathersbusiness.com)

- *Free to be You* by Elizabeth Gunter
- "Celebrating God's Design of You" CD
- "Be Blessed to be You" CD
- "Blessings from You Are Blessed in the Names of God, Volumes 1,2,3" CD set
- *Blessing Your Spirit* by Arthur Burk and Sylvia Gunter
- *You Are Blessed in the Names of God* by Sylvia Gunter
- Many other resources at this website

Sapphire Leadership Group, Inc (www.theslg.com)

- "The Redemptive Gifts of Individuals" CD set by Arthur Burk
- *Alive with Passion and Purpose* by Sandy Landry
- "Majesty of His Artistry" CD set by Arthur Burk
- Many other resources at this website

Free to Be Ministries (www.freetobeministries.com)

- *Designed for Fulfillment* by Charles Wale
- This resource is also available at www.msrepairersofthebreach.com

Endnotes

[1] Arthur Burk, Sapphire Leadership Group, Inc © Sapphire Leadership Group, Inc

[2] www.birds.cornell.edu/AllAboutBirds/studying/birdsongs

[3] Arthur Burk, Sapphire Leadership Group, Inc © Sapphire Leadership Group, Inc

[4] www.tworiversblog.com

Made in the USA
San Bernardino, CA
18 June 2017